The Parent's Guide to Primary School

Wendy Bray

Series Editor: Steve Chalke

Illustrated by John Byrne

Hodder & Stoughton
LONDON SYDNEY AUCKLAND

Copyright © 2003 by Parentalk and Wendy Bray
Illustrations copyright © 2003 by Parentalk

First published in Great Britain in 2003

The right of Wendy Bray to be identified as the Author of the
Work has been asserted by her in accordance with
the Copyright, Designs and Patents Act 1988.

10 9 8 7 6 5 4 3 2 1

All rights reserved. No part of this publication may be
reproduced, stored in a retrieval system, or transmitted,
in any form or by any means without the prior written permission
of the publisher, nor be otherwise circulated in any form of binding
or cover other than that in which it is published and without a
similar condition being imposed on the subsequent purchaser.

British Library Cataloguing in Publication Data
A record for this book is available from the British Library

ISBN 0 340 86122 3

Typeset in Sabon by Avon DataSet Ltd,
Bidford-on-Avon, Warwickshire

Printed and bound in Great Britain by
Bookmarque Ltd, Croydon, Surrey

The paper and board used in this paperback are natural recyclable products
made from wood grown in sustainable forests. The manufacturing processes
conform to the environmental regulations of the country of origin.

Hodder and Stoughton
A Division of Hodder Headline Ltd
338 Euston Road
London NW1 3BH
www.madaboutbooks.com

Contents

Acknowledgements	vii
Introduction *'Line Up Here, Please...'*	1
1 'I'm Going to BIG School!' *Getting Ready for Primary School Entry*	7
2 'Don't Forget Your Lunchbox...' *The First Weeks*	29
3 'What Did You Do at School Today?' *Understanding the Curriculum*	47
4 Bringing School Home *Nurturing a Home–School Relationship*	73
5 'Teacher Says...' *Who's Who and What's What at School*	95
6 Testing Times *The When, Where and Why of Primary School Tests*	115
7 'The Best Days of Our Lives'? *What to Do When There's a Problem*	133

8 'As Well as Can Be Expected'
  Special Educational and Medical Needs   153
9 Eleven Plus
  What Comes Next?   171

Notes   189
What It All Means: A Glossary of Terms in Primary
   Education   191
Further Information   199

Acknowledgements

Writing this book has been like taking a trip down memory lane. I have travelled through my Primary School Days as a child, teacher and mum, and have been reminded just how their unique detail has been woven together in my memory. But I could not have taken that journey, or prepared these pages, without the interest and help of friends, family, and even those whom I have never met.

So, many thanks to Dick Whittington at West Kent Area Education Office, who helped me at the very beginning of the research stage of the journey. Also to Jo Hazelwood and colleagues at the DfES, who answered my questions and tirelessly located documents and legislation when I just didn't know where to look.

Thank you to Alison, Alice and Gwen, and to David Butler at the NCPTA who made various suggestions, asked questions and read the words once they hit the page.

And of course to Tim, Maggie and Sophia at Parentalk, for your guidance, friendship, good advice and excellent editing skills ('Another snappy title, Tim?!').

The Parentalk Guide to Primary School

It has been – as always – fun and a joy to work with you.

Last but by no means least, a thankyou hug to Richard (the husband) and Lois and Benjamin (the kids) who have grown used to frequent late or non-existent suppers, and a laptop computer almost permanently fixed to the kitchen table and who never moan about either.

This book is dedicated to Margaret Sibson, my very first infant teacher, with whom I am still in touch, and is for every parent who ever waved goodbye at the classroom door, blinked back a tear and swallowed hard.

Wendy Bray
2003

Introduction

Line Up Here, Please . . .

Most of us have at least one abiding memory of our primary school.

For many it's the smell! A mix of floor polish, disinfectant and overcooked cabbage. It fills our memories in the same way that it filled the school hall during assembly, as we sat cross legged in a stiff school shirt and shiny new shoes. Our eyes were fixed alternately on 'the big boys' and the teacher bashing out 'All Things Bright and Beautiful' on a tuneless piano.

For some of us, those memories will be painful or humiliating and will have etched the pattern from which our whole school career took its shape. We may have begun to believe, from those early days, that school really wasn't our scene, or learnt to keep our heads down in order to avoid the

The Parentalk Guide to Primary School

bullies – some of whom may even have been the teachers. Others will have nothing but the sunny days locked away in the vaults of memory, and just the sound of children's voices in the playground as we pass will unlock them. Then we'll be transported back to skipping games and school sports days, stories on the carpet and cutting paper lanterns out of crisp red paper to take home at Christmas. For most, the memories will be a mix of rough and smooth, pride and embarrassment, fear and fun.

Take some time to think back over the years. What is it you remember most about your first years at school? My clearest memory is of Miss Sibson playing the piano as we learnt 'Kookaburra Sings', and shivering in my flimsy PE kit as I ran across the playground to the school hall for PE in the middle of winter! Hanging up my navy gabardine raincoat every morning on a black wire peg under a sticker decorated with a picture of a dripping pink umbrella. I longed for one just like it.

I remember the privilege of being allowed to look after Miss Cornwall's string of heavy, creamy pearls while she taught swimming in the tiny school swimming pool. I'd had pneumonia and wasn't allowed to go. This great honour made up for it.

And Mr Silleto, the headmaster, playing 'Who Can See the Wind?' on the piano as we marched silently into assembly and 'The Planet Suite' on a wooden-cased 'record player', as we marched out.

Those days can seem at one moment like a million years ago and at another like last Thursday. But when my own children started school those memories lined up together and did a forward flip across the years, in transformation.

Introduction

Suddenly, it was *my* child who was hanging up their coat in the cloakroom and doing PE in the hall, and – because you're reading this book – it's likely that it's now your child or grandchild, or someone you take care of, who is about to do the same.

'Will it have changed much?' you wonder as you contemplate that day when you'll watch your 'baby' disappear through its doors for the first time. 'Is there anything I can do to make it easier for them than it was for me?'

This book is to let you know that it has, and there is. It's written to reassure you that, if the last time you walked into a primary school building was nearly twenty years ago, an awful lot has changed in your absence – and most of it for the better.

Even if you still carry the inadequacies of those early days of formal learning, you may find that you rediscover some happy memories too. And it's those memories that we want to build for children as they begin their journey through school: a journey that promises to be a Big Adventure.

So view this book as a travel guide. It will accompany you on that journey through the primary school – from your perspective as well as the children's – because this is *your* Big Adventure too.

oOoOo

In the 1944 Education Act, Education Minister Mr Butler declared that every child should be educated at school 'or otherwise'. For a minority, the 'otherwise' path – home schooling – is a perfectly viable choice, but for the majority of children

The Parentalk Guide to Primary School

the first five to six years of 'education' will take place within the primary school community.

It's this community you'll be taken into on the pages that follow as we consider:

- what a child's experience is likely to be – and yours as parent, or carer;
- what happens in school and why – plus the questions you might ask;
- what the school should do – for each child and for you;
- how you can help – what your role and responsibility is.

Along the way we'll hear from other parents and children who've 'been there, done that' – including me and mine! My children – Lois and Benjamin – are both teenagers now, but those early days don't seem so very far away. Neither are the years I spent teaching primary school children and reassuring their parents that they – and their children – really would turn out OK in the end!

So together let's share the memories of each other's school days and swap ideas to help with the practicalities of being the parent or carer of a primary school child.

Who, Where and What?

Teachers will be referred to throughout as 'her'. I promise I'm not ignoring the excellent job male primary school teachers do. But the simple fact is there are more women than men in primary education, so most of our dealings will be with Mrs

Introduction

Always or Miss Management and their colleagues. To redress the balance and to let the boys get their elbows on the pages, children will be referred to as 'he'.

I will also generally address my words to parents, simply because the majority of those who guide children through school are parents. But if you are a grandparent or carer, know that I am including you too, and am acknowledging the special relationship you have with the child in your care.

The term 'primary school' will be used generally to cover all variations of education provision – state and independent – from four to eleven years in England, Scotland and Wales with specific exceptions (e.g. ages five to twelve in Scotland). General principles remain the same for pupils north of the border, but specific differences relating to Scottish schools and curriculum can be obtained from the Scottish Executive Education Department, and information on regional variations in Wales, particularly relating to Welsh Language teaching can be obtained from the Welsh Office Education Department (see Further Information).

There isn't space to include local variations of policy that you might find in your community, neither is there space to include great detail of curriculum areas. Other publications do that excellently, and some are referred to in the 'Further Information' section, together with websites and useful reading.

Education can be mystifying, not least because it seems to use a language all of its own. We can stumble and stutter over SATS and SENCOs and feel as if we're entering a foreign country rather than a classroom. So I've included a 'What It All Means' section – a glossary – to explain some of those mystifying titles and terms that tangle your tongue.

The Parentalk Guide to Primary School

And because there are always too many questions and not enough answers, I've asked some parents whose children are just about to start school what they always wanted to know but never liked to ask. Hopefully, *your* burning question will be smouldering there, with an answer alongside.

The pages that follow are designed to give you confidence as you navigate all that lies ahead on the Big Adventure, from first-day blues, through first-night nerves (Parents' Night that is), up homework hill and on to the edge of the primary world and beyond, where secondary school beckons.

So line up here, please . . .

'I'm Going to BIG School!'

Getting Ready for Primary School Entry

Some time ago you probably pushed your toddler in a buggy past the doors of your local primary school and considered how far off his stepping through those doors seemed to be. Perhaps more recently you've stood at the playground edge with a friend whose child is already enjoying life at 'Big School', looked down at your own child and realised that the all-important step is suddenly very much closer. It's time to think about school.

The Parentalk Guide to Primary School

Myths and Legends

There are certainly myths and legends concerning fathers who have staggered from the maternity ward to the pub to celebrate the birth of their child. Those legends tell us that they stop only to make that important phone call to St Florence's School For Fabulous Five-Year-Olds to 'put their child's name down'. But in the real world it's unlikely that you'll need to start thinking about your choice of primary school until your child is around the age of three.

If you're thinking of moving into an area purely in the hope of a child attending a particular school, find out about admissions criteria before looking for a home. Things aren't always what they seem, especially where the importance of 'catchment areas' (the area from which pupils are drawn) is concerned. You may have to rethink the maternity ward story and pop into your local school on the way to the estate agents!

Very often, the first serious look at primary education that's more than a glance across the playground is taken around the time a child begins playgroup or nursery school. At this stage, it's useful to think about the geography and social science of home, playgroup and school, as well as the maths. In other words, consider how long it will take you to leg it up that hill with a double buggy to pick your five-year-old up from school after collecting your toddler from nursery, the nappies from Sainsbury's, and before delivering said five-year-old to gym.

We're talking energy and sanity here, so it's worth having a good think about the logistics! It's usually best if you can walk with your child to school, and you may need to be close to

'I'm Going to BIG School!'

playgroups, childminders or work. Add to that the necessity of having friends – yours as well as the children's – nearby, and the value of your own community knowledge, and a local school will generally come out on top.

And then there's the philosophy and politics behind the decision – and before you think it seems as if it's you that's about to go to school, let me explain that choosing a school is likely to be one of the most important life decisions you make for your child.

But try not to panic!

 **Top Tip:** You can never find out too much about a school you might choose – ask everyone about everything!

Listen to the views of friends and family. But while you listen keep an open mind. Remember that they are sharing their own personal perspective. Doubtless it's well meant, but it could be outdated or inaccurate information. Miss Rogers 'the dragon' – with her green cardigan to match – may no longer stalk the hallways threatening to breathe the fire of her wrath on anyone, whether or not they are called George. And it might have been 1966 that the outside loos flooded badly, damaging the fabric of the main building almost beyond repair. The loos may still flood – but they are more than likely *inside*, now.

The challenge is to find a clear, true and uncluttered perspective. A perspective based on the needs of your child, yourself and the rest of your family.

The Parentalk Guide to Primary School

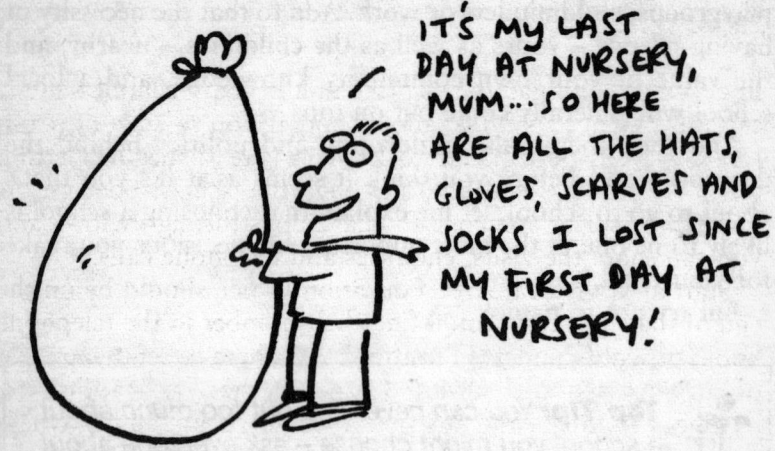

Nursery, playgroup and pre-school activities will probably have given you links with other parents, many of whom already have children at school locally and, through them, you will also have developed your own picture of the schools in your area. You may already have decided which one you'd like your child to go to. Even if you have, it's a good idea to look at one or two other schools before you make a final decision, just to be able to make comparisons. You may want to consider a school that has a religious affiliation, or weigh up the benefits of an independent fee-paying school.

It's also worth checking to make sure your child has a good chance of being admitted to the school you like. Admissions criteria are often tight and specific – especially in areas where there are a large number of families. It may not be worth applying if there's little chance of being accepted.

'I'm Going to BIG School!'

Where Do I Start?

In choosing, and gaining, a place in a primary school there is certainly plenty to think about, and if you're starting from scratch it can be difficult to know where to begin. Getting together with a friend who's in the same school boat means that there will be someone to chat things through with – and you can share the visits, enquiries and telephone calls.

Staff at your local Area Education Office should be on the end of that first call. You'll find their number in the telephone book, probably under 'Education'. Ask them to send you a list of primary schools in your area, together with addresses, telephone numbers and any special details, for example, where the boundaries of a school 'catchment' area lie and whether the school admits children who live outside that area. Or perhaps, as is the case in some schools with a religious affiliation, priority is given to families of a particular faith.

Often, schools work on a points system. For example, children living in the school catchment area score 3, and those with a brother or sister at the school score 2. So, sometimes it's a case of the higher your total 'score' the more chance your child has of being allocated a place. This may sound like a television quiz show, but it is probably the fairest way to allocate places.

Area Education Office staff will also tell you how soon you'll need to register your interest in a place. Sometimes you can apply when your child is as young as three, but you should certainly not apply later than the year before his fifth birthday – or earlier if your area admits children to full-time education at age four. It's always worth ringing the school to clarify details

The Parentalk Guide to Primary School

and to make sure that the information you have is bang up to date.

However far off it may seem at this point, find out where children will go once their primary education is complete. It's a fact of life that secondary school has a knack of coming around faster than primary school did!

If you want to consider an independent school, details can be found from Edubase, telephone 0870 120 2527 or email helpdesk@edubase.gov.uk.

Once you have made a 'shortlist' of schools you'd like to find out more about, check to see if they have recently received an OFSTED inspection. All schools in England and Wales are required to be inspected through OFSTED once every four to six years, and reports on those inspections giving details of strengths and weaknesses, are available for you to read in your local library, from the school itself, or on the Internet (www.ofsted.gov.uk). Schools in Scotland are inspected by HM Inspectors, working as part of an executive agency of the Scottish Executive Education Department.

Bear in mind that each school produces an 'Action Plan' as a result of an OFSTED inspection, and might already be well on the way to addressing any weaknesses that were identified.

More about school inspections is included in Chapter Six, 'Testing Times'.

Visiting Schools

Once you have your shortlist of three or four schools, telephone each one and ask for a copy of their brochure or prospectus.

'I'm Going to BIG School!'

This, sometimes quite glossy, booklet will tell you about the history of the school, its teaching staff, the school 'ethos' – what's important to the school community as a whole – and something about the way the school is run. It will also cover what children can be expected to learn and some points of 'policy'. For example, what the school does about homework, and whether the children wear uniform.

Bear in mind that an impressive school brochure often says more about the person who wrote and designed the brochure than the school itself. So use the brochure as a guide, not as a substitute for a visit and hard thinking. Read it carefully, making a note of anything you'd like to know more about and then ring the school to make an appointment to look round. You may have to wait a while for an appointment – but don't be discouraged. There's always a lot happening in schools, and the head teacher will want to choose a time when you can gain a balanced impression. Go with a friend or partner so that you can discuss things later – and take your child, if he is old enough to be meaningfully involved. It might be best to leave babies and toddlers with a friend.

What to Look for on a School Visit
Always visit during a normal school day and ask yourself:

- Was I given a warm welcome by reception staff, head teacher and children?
- Is there a calm working environment?
- How do the teachers and children speak to each other? Is there a sense of mutual respect, interest and care?

The Parentalk Guide to Primary School

- How is the children's work displayed on the walls? Are the displays new and up to date or faded and dog-eared?
- Is there a sense of pride in the school and in the shared 'purpose' of the school community?
- Do the children appear relaxed and happy?
- Are they occupied and absorbed by their work, or are they sitting around looking bored?
- What is the standard of that work? Are the children happy to share their tasks with you or explain them with enthusiasm?
- Are they encouraged to think for themselves and ask questions – perhaps risking a wrong answer in a safe environment? Do they listen to each other?
- Is there a good balance of work from books, practical tasks and listening to an adult?
- Does the head teacher talk about pastoral issues and teaching style as well as policy?
- Can you hear children – and staff – laughing from time to time?

If you have the opportunity to talk to the head teacher, you might like to ask:

- how Maths, and Literacy (reading and writing skills) are taught and enjoyed;
- what the school's discipline (behaviour) and bullying policy outlines (a good school should have both);
- how parents are involved in the life of the school;
- where the children play and do PE;
- how many pupils are in each class, and how many staff teach them;

'I'm Going to BIG School!'

- how Religious Education, Personal Health and Social Education are taught;
- what the lunchtime arrangements are: hot dinners and/or packed lunches;
- if the school fosters any links with secondary schools and the local community;
- for admissions criteria to be clarified.

Eventually, a subtle combination of folklore, friends, your own 'gut' feelings, and facts will help you make a choice. Out of the fog of indecision, the school you'd really like your child to go to will appear. Try to see it as your Number One rather than your One and Only – admission isn't certain yet.

Then, following the advice the school has given you, apply. Whatever you do, never assume that your local school will have a place for your child by rights.

'I've Chosen the School – How Do I Get My Child In?'

It's wise to apply to more than one school – so choose a Number Two and Three – even if you have set your heart on your Number One. And *always* apply to your local school, even if you're not keen on what you've seen or heard and it's right down there at Number Seven.

When my daughter was about to start school I discovered that parents from a mile or so away applied to the school in our area because they thought it was better than the one in their own. Whilst parents in our area were applying to the school in theirs for the same reason! We can assume that the grass is

The Parentalk Guide to Primary School

greener in the other school field, or that there is some kind of 'kudos' in driving our child to the 'better' school elsewhere. The 'better' school could be the one on your doorstep.

As many schools are oversubscribed – a simple question of too many children wanting too few places – allocation of places often depends on the catchment area. Simply how close you live to the school can make a difference. Should all else fail, applying to your local school at least means there'll be a place for your child somewhere.

Allocating places can be a real headache for head teachers. About six months before my son was due to begin school I heard a rumour that places would be limited. I had applied for a place when his sister had started two years before, but I knew there were no guarantees. So I went to see the head teacher, and she showed me three piles of cards: a pile of 'probably nots', a pile of 'maybes' and a pile of just three 'definites'. My son was the first of the three 'definites', the boy next door the second, and a child who lived in the street at the end of the school playground, the third. Each had a brother or sister already at the school. The head teacher explained that the 'maybes' consisted of children who all had roughly equal 'scores' and so equal 'rights' to a place.

That evening she was planning to sit down with an advisor from the Local Education Authority to allocate places as fairly as possible. As I left, I wondered just how long it would take. I didn't envy her the task. If you really feel you want to pursue a place at a particular school, you can appeal against a school's decision. Your Area Education Office will tell you how. You can also read the School Admissions Appeals Code of Practice to give you an idea of the procedure (see Further Information).

'I'm Going to BIG School!'

There are enormous regional and local variations in schools applications and admissions. Some LEAs discourage parents from applying for a place at more than one school at a time, so always check local folklore, LEA recommendations – *and* your entitlements. They might not match.

Bear in mind that schools can only hold so many pupils, and will have made a commitment to keep class sizes down. Also remember that appeals procedures can be stressful. Think carefully about whether you really want to go ahead with the extensive negotiations and uncertainty involved before you begin. It's perhaps wisest to make a reasonable choice in the first place based on a wide range of criteria, than for a first experience of school to involve the stress that is inevitably linked to an appeal.

A number of children end up in schools their parents would never have chosen first, but now happily – and with great relief – admit have suited them wonderfully. It's reassuring to know that children have an uncanny knack of making the most of wherever they go to school.

> **Top Tip:** Try to keep an open mind about where they'll go to school – your first choice may not necessarily be the best choice.

As parents, our attitude is crucial. Children look to us for guidance as to how they should feel about most things at this early age. Like the spider that suddenly appears in the bathtub – if we shriek at the thought of it, let alone the sight, chances

The Parentalk Guide to Primary School

are they will too. The same goes for their attitude to school. If you don't get your first choice school, always talk positively to your child about the school they'll finally go to – even if it's your Number Seven. Children should not feel that they are being short-changed before they start.

When you do finally receive an offer of a place, accept it – by letter – and file your offer and a copy of your acceptance away safely. It may be worth making a file marked 'school' – as the years go by you'll have plenty of things to go in it.

The day you receive confirmation of a place in a school is an important day, so mark it in some way and show your child that starting the Big Adventure of school is something worth celebrating.

Before You Go . . .

Go to any introductory meetings the school may hold for parents of new entrants, and find out everything you can about what will happen in your child's first few days there. If you feel confident and enthusiastic, your child will very likely 'catch' that confidence and enthusiasm and make it his own.

Make sure he has everything he needs in terms of uniform (if it's worn) and equipment. Some schools run excellent 'Hand On' shops for uniform that help with the cost. He will probably not need an enormous pencil case filled with a slide rule, a scientific calculator and two hundred multicoloured felt pens. The teacher will tell you what's really needed.

Don't miss any special New Entrant days for children. They will get to walk the route to their classroom, find the toilet, the

'I'm Going to BIG School!'

coat pegs, even the Lost Property bin. Believe it or not, that's exciting! And it helps them (and you) become familiar with the most important routines and landmarks before they start. Most schools arrange for children to spend at least an afternoon or morning with their new classmates – sometimes for several weeks – just having fun and finding at least the toes of their feet! But, more about how that's organised later.

> **Top Tip:** Thirstily absorb all the information the school can give you before your child starts – it will build your confidence – and his.

If you are very lucky you may receive a home visit from your child's class teacher before the start of term. This is an opportunity for you to meet each other literally on home ground, and for all of you to build the foundations of a home/school relationship.

The school will also arrange for you to take your child along to meet a doctor linked with the school to discuss any health or medical needs he may have in school. (These are discussed further in the chapter 'As Well as Can Be Expected'.)

A Friend to Go with . . .

I can remember starting school firmly clasping the hand of my friend Gill. We went everywhere together, and I believe we made a difference for each other. I'm still much the same. It's a whole

19

lot easier starting something new with a friend. Whether it's first night at the gym (very unlikely) or a wine tasting (much more likely!) I always feel more confident if I've brought a friend along.

A beauty parlour near us once ran a whole marketing campaign on just that kind of reassurance. It was a 'wax four legs for the price of two' offer. Unless they were diversifying into dog grooming, they had obviously learnt the lesson that where anything's slightly daunting or downright terrifying, it's better with a buddy. And if it's true for an adult, how much more must that be so for children starting school?

Schools are usually happy to place friends together, and will very probably ask if a child has a special friend, perhaps from pre-school. But even if children do start school alone, it will probably not be long – possibly only minutes – before they have found a friend from whom they will seem inseparable for the rest of their days! The class teacher will have each child's best interests at heart, and will do her best from the very beginning to ensure that none are isolated.

If you think it would help, invite a soon-to-be classmate to tea a few times beforehand. But don't force friendships – they'll develop naturally. Children generally cope better than we imagine – and certainly better than us on the first night at the gym!

 **Top Tip:** Support and encourage the new friendships your child makes. They could be a lifeline – and last a lifetime!

'I'm Going to BIG School!'

If you have twins, triplets or beyond you will need to make a decision, along with the head teacher, about whether they should begin school in the same class. Each might thrive in a class of their own where they can make their own friends and develop their unique personality, especially if they have a tendency to rely on each other too much, or might resist making the effort required to make friends. But, equally, brothers and sisters might settle more quickly and gain comfort from each other's presence. You'll know your children best, and the teacher will know class organisation best, so decide together, remembering that smaller schools may not be able to offer you a choice.

First Class Education

'Foundation' classes (sometimes called Reception) in which children start their school career vary, but all will follow a similar Foundation or 'Early Years' curriculum. Some schools stagger entry throughout the year allowing a class to build itself through two or even three intakes of new entrants. Others work with half a class of new entrants in each session (morning and afternoon) for the first few weeks to allow children to 'find the remainder of their feet' in a smaller group.

Since September 2001, no infant class (up to age seven) with a single teacher has been allowed to contain more than thirty pupils. Most primary school classes, including those at junior level (ages seven to eleven), will vary in size from around twenty-two to thirty-five pupils, with schools making a commitment to keep their class sizes as small as possible.

Some teachers work in what is called a 'team teaching' or 'shared responsibility' setting. 'Team teaching' involves a large class of children being managed by two or more teachers working together. Children are taught through a blend of whole class and small group work in a much larger open-plan space, or in adjoining teaching areas. So don't be surprised if the class thrives on what might look to the untrained eye like organised chaos – it does work, and often works very well indeed.

Teachers who share expertise can offer a special quality and flexibility of learning experience. Staff in a year-group team, and subject specialists (for example, in music or PE) may also choose to work in this way.

Infant classes will almost always have the support of at least one Teaching Assistant (TA), often called a Learning Support Assistant (LSA), who assists the teacher. A 'TA' or 'LSA' will also give support on a one-to-one basis to children with special educational needs, either for all or part of the school day.

 ***Top Tip:*** *If something about school organisation mystifies you – ask about it.*

Most of the children's learning activities take place in the classroom setting. But they will also use the school hall for PE, Games, assemblies and some Music and Arts events and, if they're lucky, they'll also have a library, and specialist Art, Computer or Music rooms. They'll also sometimes move to other classes to share working areas or equipment.

'I'm Going to BIG School!'

Occasionally they may leave the school in well-supervised small groups on a visit in the local community, to museums, for sporting events or for other school trips. Parents must always give their written consent in advance – usually by signing a form – and will very possibly be asked to lend a hand on the day. Go along if you can – you'll enjoy it – and may even learn as much as the children! Chapter Seven, 'The Best Days . . . ?', has more about school trips.

School can be loud, busy and confusing for a new entrant, so experience of pre-school groups helps to ease transition into this busy community. And there are a number of other ways in which parents can help.

'What Can I Do to Help My Child Start School "Well"?'

As parents we can spend so much time on the academic side of preparation – buying pre-school workbooks and teaching our children to count – that we risk neglecting the very skills that academic tasks depend on for success: skills like listening, sitting still (harder than we think!), following instructions, and just the business of looking after 'me'. These skills carry children from the beginning to the end of the school day with growing confidence, enjoyment and independence, so they are worth spending time on.

Any pre-school 'schoolwork' tasks at home need to be fun. Just as much can be learnt from ordinary daily activities: shopping, cooking, sharing books together, chatting about life, exploring the local environment and just, well, *playing* together.

The Parentalk Guide to Primary School

Top Tip: *Before your child begins school, spend some time together on quiet games and activities that take a bit of concentration – they are good preparation for working at school.*

Try not to plan any major changes to coincide with children starting school. Especially – and I know it's difficult – the arrival of a new baby or a house move. Children can sometimes be disturbed by a baby arriving as they start school, and may become quite convinced that they have been 'pushed out' to make room! Of course, we can't always engineer things exactly – but we should certainly try to bear their feelings in mind. If at all possible, your returning to work or changing jobs should also wait until you know your child is settled.

However much you know you'll miss him once he starts school, try not to tell him too often – and certainly don't shed tears over it in front of him. It's unfair to expect children to understand the parental emotions entwined with their first day at school. And it doesn't hurt to give the impression that life at home has been an awful lot more boring than his life at school – he won't want to feel he's missed something while he's been away!

Top Tip: *Don't underestimate the emotional upheaval of starting school – for you more than your child!*

'I'm Going to BIG School!'

> THERE MIGHT BE TEARS ON YOUR FIRST DAY AT SCHOOL...

> DON'T WORRY MUM... YOU CAN BORROW MY HANKY.

Every child needs a secure, unchanging and dependable base from which to launch themselves into their new world. Home will be a refuge.

Fliss and Terry decided to transform their daughter Aimee's bedroom from a toddler's room to a 'grown-up schoolgirl's room' as a surprise while she enjoyed her first day at school. They thought it would encourage her to have a new desk and bed combined, plain curtains rather than Teddy ones and a brand new desk lamp instead of sheep dancing round a field.

But she was distraught at the change, and Terry spent the evening moving teddies, sheep and toddler bed back while Fliss consoled a confused Aimee. She welcomed everything new eventually, and even had some ideas of her own (!) but she needed her familiar refuge for those first few months. Fliss and Terry were just glad they hadn't changed the paintwork and carpet!

The Parentalk Guide to Primary School

 **Top Tip:** Don't give the impression that everything will change because of school. Reassure them that most of the old familiar things will stay the same.

It's a good idea to continue with established hobbies and clubs, even if they may need to be given up once the school routine makes other demands. Children need to know that things at home will remain the same and that the friends, toys and activities they enjoyed before school will continue – but that school will add new ones too!

Above all adults need to talk enthusiastically, calmly and realistically about school. Try to avoid promising – accidentally or otherwise – what you're not sure will be delivered and encourage children to take school in their stride.

'What Should My Child Be Able to Do Before He Starts School?'

It helps enormously if your child can be as independent as possible in school, so ask yourself if he can do the following:

- carry a small tray or single items of food and drink responsibly;
- eat with others and use cutlery (Can he open and close his lunch box, or undo a Penguin wrapper? Or do you always do it for him?);
- go to the toilet and wash and dry his hands by himself (Has

'I'm Going to BIG School!'

he ever used a paper towel, for instance? Has your son ever used a urinal?);
- fasten shoes, preferably with Velcro or easy buckles to begin with, identifying left from right (Draw or write inside his shoes and teach him to make an 'L' shape with his left hand held vertically and flat and thumb pointing right and match it to the 'L' in their shoe – Left hand, Left shape, Left shoe.);
- button or zip his coat, and dress and undress fairly quickly and effectively (Make it fun – play a game with a stopwatch, timing him to see if he can 'break the record' each evening for a while before he starts school.);
- use and carry simple scissors, pencils, brushes, safely, and handle books with respect;
- understand, remember and follow simple instructions including some details (Try it out when shopping in the supermarket: 'Can you find the chocolate biscuits in the blue packet with the ship on, and bring me two packets?' Or begin to give him a few, short but more complex chores at home: 'Would you take this pile of laundry upstairs, and put the socks in your drawer and the towels in the big bathroom cupboard?');
- sit still and listen for short periods, take turns, queue, wait patiently, and know not to interrupt (Sitting to listen to stories from you and story tapes will help.);
- ask and answer questions about routines and activities (Teach him to ask questions like, 'Can you help me, please?');
- play co-operatively with others, moderating voice and activity when requested;
- be polite and show consideration for others.

The Parentalk Guide to Primary School

... And while you wait for the Big Day to come, be reassured that there are more ways than one to be embarrassed by your child's admission to school.

Sarah had just started school and had, like most children her age, needed to avail herself of a fresh pair of knickers from the 'emergency knickers box' kept under Miss Deverold's table. They were duly washed at home, and the next morning, when Sarah boarded the bus to school with her dad, she was delighted to see Miss Deverold sitting at the back. Overwhelmed with delight at the sight of her new heroine, and wanting to impress her teacher with her reliability, Sarah shouted, 'Don't worry, Miss Deverold, my dad's got your knickers in his pocket!'[1]

'Don't Forget Your Lunchbox...'

The First Weeks

The First Day

A friend of mine tells the story of a little lad who, on arriving at school on his first day, asked his mum tearfully, 'How long have I got to be here for?' His mum, looking ahead epically to the future, replied, 'Oh! For the next sixteen years or so, darling!'

My friend comments, 'Poor little tot thought he was going home at quarter past three!'

For me, that story pretty neatly sums up the different way parents and children look at that first day of school. For parents it's a huge fanfare-blowing, psyche-rattling 'moment'. For kids, it is just school. Excited school; 'can't wait' school; 'So this is what it's all about' school; but nevertheless, just *school* – and just for *today*.

And like the little boy who woke up on the second day and said, 'Do you mean I have to go *again today*?' most children will handle it one day at a time. A sensible philosophy for parents too, considering the twelve or so years ahead that we focus on!

Every school makes special arrangements for the first few days. Children may be at school for one day a week at first, for morning or afternoon sessions, or go home for lunch – just to begin with. These arrangements may seem complicated, inconvenient, or just plain exhausting but go along happily with them if you can. The schools know how to help children make the best start. Trust them and be patient – even when you've walked the route to school and back ten times so far this week and it's only Tuesday!

Whenever and however the time comes, most children will walk through the classroom door almost without looking back, anxious to get on with it all. Some will shed a few tears en route to school, or mention a knot in their stomachs. Very few will be really distressed. The good thing is, teachers are experienced players in every possible scenario.

If you get there on time and appear calm and happy – however nervous and emotional you feel – it will make all the difference. So, try out the walk to school at school time the week before, and try to make the early morning at home well planned and calm – at least, as far as possible!

On the first day, be prepared for an alarm call, in the form of one small child dressed in uniform and clutching a school bag – at 5 a.m! My daughter sat herself down by the front door dressed and ready, half an hour early on her first day, annoyed that I had not woken up the caretaker, so that she could get into school and get – what she called – 'orgnised'.

Her reception class teacher confirmed at the end of the week, that she was indeed 'orgnised', and had also tried to 'orgnise' the rest of the school!

I should probably also point out that the same daughter is now sixteen, and the word 'orgnised' – or even organised – does not appear in her vocabulary. As a parent, it's worth remembering that 'This too will pass'.

Saying Goodbye

Make arrangements so that you can take your child to school yourself, at the very least, on the first day. This is a special day to share. As you walk to school remind him how the day will go and when you will meet up again. It might help to tie the 'when' into the 'what' through reference to other familiar activities he knows *you* do, as well as the things he'll do.

'When Milly's been to playgroup, we'll have lunch and wash up. I'll change the beds and put the washing in while Milly watches *CBeebies*, then we'll come up to meet you.'

Reassure him about how and where you'll meet him. Something like, 'Mrs Evans will bring you out to the playground and I'll be standing with Milly by the red gate.'

The Parentalk Guide to Primary School

> **Top Tip:** The first day at school is an important day in life – but not the most important day. Try not to turn it into a tragi-comic drama.

'How Do I Say "Goodbye"?'

When you arrive at school on the first morning, follow the routine the teacher has suggested. Help him hang up his coat and find a friend. Then say something like, 'Have a lovely day, I'll see you later!' before giving him a hug and a kiss, and *leaving*. Don't go for long cuddles. It's these that will make the tears flow if they're ready to. Just let him know you're going, remind him about your meeting up later, and slip quietly away. It's the parting that can be hard, so try not to draw it out.

Resist the temptation to bang on the window and wave when you get outside, or to hang around at the edge of the playground or in the car down the road to 'see if he is alright'. If he sees you, he will wonder why you need to check! And try very hard to resist the temptation to phone the school to see if he's settled. It really *is* almost always true that children are fine five minutes – often five seconds – after their parents have left. It's often the parents, not the children, who cry longest. The school will ring you if there's a problem they can't handle.

What If They're *Really* Upset?

A small number of children become very upset, especially if they're not used to being away from their parents. If this

'Don't Forget Your Lunchbox...'

happens, don't panic. There are things you can do to help. If there are just a few tears, the teacher or assistant will calmly and kindly distract him or try to involve him with other children or new activities. If he gets very upset she will try to sit with him as long as is necessary. Most importantly *you* must remain positive and calm. If you begin to be upset too, he will see his fears as justified. Again, it's a case of, 'If Mum's upset, it must be bad to be left here!'

Before you leave – *because leave you must* – reassure him firmly and calmly that you are going, but that he will be OK and that you will be back soon. Then, make your parting warm but brief – and leave the school, however hard it is.

The Parentalk Guide to Primary School

> **Top Tip:** Some schools allow children to take a small soft toy into school at first. It sometimes helps, but consider what you'll do if it gets lost – or it's never put down!

If you're feeling down or upset yourself, meet friends, go to work, get involved in a particularly absorbing task, or watch a video – anything to make the school day go faster. Then make sure you're waiting for him exactly as you said you'd be.

You will probably find that everything has been fine. He may not have been deliriously happy every moment, but he will have got used to the idea, and it will grow on him. Repeat the same routine the following day and he will soon realise, however tough it is, that school is a non-negotiable. Rely on the experience of the school. They will want children to feel happy and secure, just as much as you do.

'Don't Forget Your Lunchbox...'

The First Weeks...

The first few weeks will largely depend on the success of the first few days. The aim is for children to look forward to the school day, to walk independently into the classroom with a cheery smile and a wave, ready for what the new day will bring. Continue to make sure everything at home is 'as normal' and that any new routines have been explained – even practised – in advance (the journey to school with someone other than you, for example).

Children need encouragement to take the day 'as it comes' and to be praised when they show signs of growing independence. The trick is to avoid making them feel that we now expect them to take on the world!

> **Top Tip:** Let your child have a 'cool off and crash out time' when they get home from school. Resist the temptation to ask twenty questions.

The main focus of the first weeks will be settling into school routine. Books will be brought home to share, and perhaps some number or language work. Don't expect more than one simple 'homework' task every few days – plus time to read together. Children usually carry a notebook or homework diary between home and school. This acts as a point of contact between parent and teacher, and generally gives details about tasks set, and any problems a child might be having. It might also contain guidelines for helping with reading, numbers and writing, and following these guidelines will help everyone to work together.

My son and daughter were given special royal blue 'book bags' printed with the school logo. When I asked what the bag contained my daughter put her nose in the air and said, 'Important stuff'. She reluctantly showed me the contents, as if I really should know all about them and was just 'Silly Mummy', anyway. Both children took their book bags to bed for the first few days; such was their pride in this 'important stuff'.

'What Will the Children Do at School?'

Some schools hold 'curriculum' evenings or afternoons for new parents, when the main subjects and teaching methods are explained, and parents are given ideas of how to help at home. At Foundation level the curriculum includes activities and tasks called 'Stepping Stones to Early Learning Goals'. You may also be given some 'hands on' experience of the activities your child will enjoy at school. All in all, these meetings are not to be missed.

In the early primary years a considerable amount of time is spent sitting in a group and listening to the teacher. It can be quite tough for children who are used to 'being on the go' all day suddenly to have to tow the line, sit still and listen. It's a skill that doesn't come naturally, especially to some boys, who often prefer a more active approach to learning. Teachers – and indeed the government – are particularly aware of the struggle boys have with school-based tasks which don't match their natural 'learning style', and, as a result, a number of resources

'Don't Forget Your Lunchbox...'

> MY NEWS
>
> MUM, DAD! THIS IS MY NEWS REPORT OF THE NEWS I REPORTED WHEN IT WAS NEWS REPORTING TIME AT SCHOOL TODAY!

have been developed to help parents – especially dads – to encourage their sons and make their learning fun and relevant. If your son is particularly active or reluctant to concentrate on schoolwork, it may be worth looking out for them. (See Further Information for details.)

> **Top Tip:** When they do *talk* about school listen hard – you'll learn a lot about what really matters to them.

At some point in the first weeks children are given a Baseline Test of their skills and abilities. Individual schools may give this test different titles, but it has the same function: to give

The Parentalk Guide to Primary School

teachers a grasp of what each child can do as a useful starting point – or baseline – from which to measure progress. The test takes place as part of normal classroom activities, and as such children won't notice any difference from other 'work'. Teachers merely observe a number of key activities and make notes about the children's responses. The test is nothing to worry about, and certainly needs no preparation. (More about Baseline Tests and what they involve appears in the chapter, 'Testing Times'.)

At this stage, don't be surprised if your child fires himself out of school like a ball from a cannon or zooms around you, pokes his little sister with breathtaking ferocity, and hurtles around the playground as if on a frenzied mission. It's normal! Sitting quietly for much of the day is a strain – that excess energy has to go somewhere. Keep after-school sports activities going, or go home via your local park to let off steam safely. At the same time praise and encourage him when he does sit still and concentrate, and help him make the most of relaxing times spent sitting close to Mum, Dad or Gran to share books quietly and conversation.

Back in the New Routine

Much of a child's sense of 'being OK at school' develops from being able to cope confidently with a range of different activities: listening well, following routine and looking after himself. It's often in 'looking after me' that children struggle. For instance, some children don't like going to the toilet at school. They often become so absorbed in their activities that they

'Don't Forget Your Lunchbox...'

simply forget to go – or go before they get there! It's very common, and at least a good sign that they are concentrating on what really matters! The teacher – like Miss Deverold at the end of Chapter One – will always have some spare knickers and pants to hand, and will take little notice of the need for them, so don't let accidents bother you either.

If 'borrowing from the knickers box' becomes a bit of a *regular* event, talk to the teacher. Most staff will remind children to visit the loo as a matter of course – but an extra reminder or two might help.

Lunchtime

Children sometimes find it a challenge to eat in a huge crowd. For them it can be like being an extra in a Hollywood epic about the Feeding of the Five Thousand! They become so distracted by those around them that they eat too slowly and don't finish their food in the allotted time. If children take a packed lunch to school, parents spend time assembling a tasty lunch box, only to have it returned, almost full, at teatime.

It might help to remember the general rule about children and food – they'll eat if they're hungry. And if they are genuinely frightened of the noise and bustle they can usually be found a quiet place to eat their lunch until their confidence grows. Children should never be forced to eat, but if you are concerned that hardly a crumb passes their lips at midday from Monday to Friday, have a word with the class teacher. She will ask the Mealtime Assistant or MTA (you knew her as the 'dinner lady')

The Parentalk Guide to Primary School

to give some gentle encouragement and will let you know if there is a real problem.

Often, children who eat school meals[2] for the first time are a bit mystified by the whole process. They find it hard to identify what they're eating – or come home with tales of strange food combinations. Jack, for example, told his mum and dad he'd eaten 'cake' and then on careful lip-licking reflection, 'cake and custard'. When asked if he'd eaten any vegetables Jack looked puzzled and replied, 'They don't have vegetables'. Then, on second thoughts scraped the plate of his lunchtime memory and identified carrots, at least. Sometimes, it's just hard to spot food in a new form – especially if carrots come in tiny dark yellow cubes tasting entirely different from the long orange crunchy fingers we're used to.

> **Top Tip:** Don't think they've gone off their food if their lunch remains untouched. Chances are life is just too exciting to make time to eat!

Some schools have a 'tuck' or 'snack' time at morning break, when the children are allowed to buy something from a school-run 'tuck shop', or eat a snack brought from home. But providing a hearty breakfast might go some way to alleviate your fear that your child will faint from hunger by 3 p.m. It doesn't usually take long for them to become so swept along by friends, routine and the game they want to continue afterwards, that they discover they've eaten their lunch along with everyone else. Eating lunch at home shouldn't be an option. The lunch hour is an important part of the school day – for socialising as much as sustenance, and shouldn't be missed.

It's a Hard Day's School

Four- and five-year-olds will inevitably be very tired at the end of the school day. At five, my son sat eating his suppertime macaroni cheese, excitedly telling me about his day as I milled around the kitchen. His speech became slower and his head drooped, until suddenly his words stopped mid-sentence and I turned to find his head cheek first in his macaroni. He was sound asleep! So these first weeks are not the time for late-night outings, homework after supper, or sudden changes of plan.

> ***Top Tip:*** *Expect a tired and fractious child for much of the time during the first weeks of school. Bad behaviour shouldn't be left unchecked – but it can at least be understood.*

As mornings develop a routine of their own, it will be easier to share 'school runs' or walks with a friend. This will ease the burden for you, especially if you've got younger children, and it's a good way to begin to build children's independence safely.

Schools sometimes have a 'walking bus' scheme, whereby volunteer parents and carers form a rota to 'walk' a large group of children to school. Everyone wears a brightly coloured

The Parentalk Guide to Primary School

reflective tabard for safety, and is 'picked up' at their door or very close to home. 'Walking buses' encourage independence, teamwork and good road safety habits, and they're *fun*! (See 'Further Information' for the National Confederation of Parent Teacher Associations (NCPTA) which will have details of how to set up a 'walking bus' scheme.)

We all need time to unwind and share our day, and children are no exception – but they won't want a cross-examination. Take their lead and talk about what they want to talk about. *You* may want to know how their number work is going – *they* may want to tell you about the gurgling drain outside Miss Bludgeon's art room. Try to become fascinated. If you stay interested in the gurgle of drains, the really valuable stuff will follow. And don't be surprised if, when you ask, 'What did you do at school today?' you get the answer, 'Stuff' or 'Nothing'. That's OK. The fact that they don't want to elaborate doesn't necessarily mean they want to leave school permanently tomorrow. It just means they've given all their energy to this place today, thank you very much, Dad, and have now had enough.

What Did You Say?

Neither are these early school weeks the time to expect children to be on their best behaviour at home! Life has changed. They're learning to cope with a whole range of new activities and influences, and these take some balancing. They're bound to get a bit wobbly sometimes. One of the wobbles parents notice most is the choice of a few colourful words they'd rather weren't included in the family vocabulary.

'Don't Forget Your Lunchbox...'

Children are playing and working alongside classmates from a wide range of different backgrounds and family style. It's part of the richness of the school experience! But bad language might be the 'fallout'. If an offending word pops out, you could just stop the chat mid-flow or point the word out calmly and say, 'We don't say that at home.' Then explain why (that bit's up to you!) without condemning the child the word might have been learnt from. If bad language stays – and you'd rather it left – mention it, in a low-key way, to the teacher. She'll probably have a good idea of its source and will try to stem the flow. The trouble is, children often genuinely don't know that the word they've used is offensive, or will use a word to get a reaction, so sometimes it's just best to ignore it.

We tried to ignore a word the first time, mildly say 'Not here, thanks' on the second utterance and get pretty cross in a disappointed kind of way, on the third. It usually worked. Never blame another child or parent or imply that 'school has made you naughty'.

Whatever the behaviour, stay firm and understanding. This Jekyll-and-Hyde phase doesn't last long. Children will usually get back to being themselves pretty quickly.

> ***Top Tip:*** *Suddenly 'Teacher' becomes all-important and knows everything. This might mean that Mum and Dad don't. Don't worry – enjoy some time off!*

The Parentalk Guide to Primary School

Getting On Together

Making friends is an exciting part of these first few weeks. It might take time for friendships to form and peer groups to bond, but if children do find it hard to make friends, the teacher will usually notice, and may have some ideas to help. Strategies for building friendships need time to work. Joining an out of school club or inviting a classmate home for supper might help.

Keep in occasional 'passing' contact with the class teacher. If you do have a concern mention it briefly before or after school, send in a short note, or call the school, so that the teacher can arrange to have a longer chat at another time. Also be sure to mention anything significant that happens at home or outside school that might have a bearing on your child's behaviour, mood, or ability to concentrate.

If a child's behaviour deteriorates in school, teachers will suggest meeting with parents to talk about it. They will also do what they can to support you if you are worried by any behaviour at home. Don't see this request as interfering or as a judgment on your parenting. Listen, give your viewpoint, share your feelings, and work out a strategy together. And certainly don't be embarrassed – the teacher will have seen it all (and lots more besides) before.

A positive and mutually supportive relationship with teachers can transform both your child's experience and *your* experience of school. Try to go out of your way to say a special 'thankyou' when things have gone well, a problem has been resolved, or children have enjoyed a special activity. Teachers need encouragement too!

Things Can Only Get Better...

As the days of the first term pass, school should become an enjoyable and vital part of life for most children, and you will find yourself breathing a sigh of relief because everything is ticking along nicely. At the same time, however, don't be surprised if you also begin to feel a bit bereft, especially if your child is the only one, or the last to go to school.

When my son started school, a friend who had already seen her three children off in the same direction and missed each one in turn, recognised my feelings. She took me out for the day, made sure I was absorbed, put up with me looking at my watch every ten minutes and delivered me back to school with fifteen minutes to spare before 'home time'. Although I was delighted for my son to be at school, I found his absence difficult for some time, and still hate the quiet house on the first day of term. I doubt I'll change. But it helped me to understand that my feelings were perfectly natural, and that I didn't need to be ashamed of them. I simply enjoyed being with my children (usually!) and missed them when I wasn't.

So, if it happens to you, get together with another parent who feels or has felt the same, and reassure yourself with the knowledge that you have completed part one of the great task of parenting. You have launched them on that good ship Big Adventure – it's just that the bottle has swung back and walloped you a bit!

I'VE BEEN SENT HOME BECAUSE OF A HEADACHE... THE HEADMASTER SAYS I'M GIVING HIM ONE.

'What Did You Do at School Today?'

Understanding the Curriculum

It's something that our kids tell us we should never say: *'And what did you do at school today?'*

The truth is, whatever they did, at the end of a long day of doing it, they don't really want to tell us about it!

When five-year-old Jack was asked by his dad, for the fifth time in his first week, what he had done at school, he looked at him with some contempt and said, 'Why do you keep asking me?' Dad, of course, wanted reassurance. Jack just wanted a bit of peace. (Isn't it good to see the occasional reversal of roles?) Maybe we need to understand that from a child's perspective, school is *their* world – and very possibly not our business at all.

The Parentalk Guide to Primary School

So because they won't tell you what they do all day, I'll try. To do so, however, inevitably means a few facts, figures and some jargon being flung in your direction. But bear with me. As a parent, you probably won't need to explore each curriculum area in depth, but you will need to know what the National Curriculum is, how it is organised, and have some idea of just what it is children do all day in following it.

'What Is the National Curriculum?'

The National Curriculum provides teachers in England and Wales with a comprehensive framework for children's formal learning between the ages of five and sixteen. In other words it tells teachers what children need to learn, how they should be taught it, and when.

The DfES (Department for Education and Skills) describe it neatly on their excellent website for parents (www.dfes.gov.uk/parents) like this:

The National Curriculum:
- Sets out the most important knowledge and skills that every child has a right to learn.
- Is a framework given to teachers by government, so that all schoolchildren are taught in a way that is balanced and manageable, but hard enough to challenge them.
- Gives standards that measure how well children are doing in each subject so teachers can plan to help them do better.

'What Did You Do at School Today?'

The framework, and the subjects within it, are taught in much the same way across the country. (Teachers in Scotland follow the very similar SEED 5–14 programme.)

Reception classes have their own Foundation Curriculum based on government guidelines called 'Curriculum Guidance for the Foundation Stage', then all primary school subjects are taught throughout the two 'Key Stages' (One and Two) that span most of a child's primary school life. Key Stage One covers school years One–Two (ages 6–7 approximately) and Key Stage Two school years Three–Six (ages 8–11 approximately).

Children work at different *levels* throughout each stage, and each level has its own 'attainment targets'. These are the key *skills, knowledge* and *understanding* which the children should be able to demonstrate at each level. For instance, in Maths, 'knowledge' might involve being able to explain what 'multiplication' means, 'skill' would involve being able to do the calculation itself, and 'understanding' would be shown by the ability to demonstrate how multiplication of numbers relates to addition and subtraction of numbers, and also how they relate to 'real life'. In other words, children will learn not only *how* to do something but why and when, too. Each subject – and stick with me on the structure, we'll get to the contents later – is taught so that children can make steady progress along an increasingly complex learning pathway.

While they are in primary school that pathway will climb up through the first two stages from age six onwards, usually climbing to another 'stage' every two years. More able children may move a little more quickly through the levels, and some

The Parentalk Guide to Primary School

children who need extra help, move a little more slowly. This means that at each Key Stage, children will be working at a number of different *levels* along the pathway and towards those different 'attainment targets' (skills, knowledge and understanding).

Key stages, levels and targets might sound like 'It's a Knockout!' but this multi-layered multi-target system is probably the best way to ensure that each child works to the best of his ability.

Appropriately enough, we could imagine the primary curriculum as a rather unusual apple from which primary pupils will get a taste of eleven different subjects – here's the content at last – with core subjects at its heart:

- English (reading, writing, speaking, listening)
- Mathematics (using maths, number, shape, measures and data)
- Science (life processes, living things, physical processes)
- Information Technology (computers)
- RE (Religious Education – not strictly part of the National Curriculum, but still required to be taught and usually treated as a core subject).

But what does that mean in practice? For example...

'How Will They Learn to Read and Write?'

Children are taught to read and write using a good balance of traditional and newly developed methods based on research

'What Did You Do at School Today?'

into what helps and what doesn't. So, whilst you'll recognise many of the reading and writing activities children do in school, others may need more explanation. A good school will offer parents the opportunity to learn more about what's being taught, especially regarding Literacy and Numeracy – in special parents' evenings. Be there if you possibly can – they'll demystify a lot!

> **Top Tip:** Never miss an opportunity to read to your children – it passes on so much more than just a story!

As they start to read and write, children spend time exploring the 'mechanics' of words and sentences and how they are put together. That's why children often 'write' scribbles as part of play before they are able to do 'the real thing'. It's an essential part of understanding what words 'do' and how they are put together to make a text.

They'll learn that a *text* isn't just something that pops up on Mum's mobile phone, but a piece of writing which could be a poem, a play, information in books or a feature on a website, as well as stories.

As they begin to look at letters, sounds and simple words they will employ a variety of 'recognition strategies', using a number of clues together, until the letter or word is recognised. That's why pointing out the names of shops and the colours, logos and trademarks that go with them is so helpful at the pre-school stage.

The Parentalk Guide to Primary School

I should have realised that my daughter would become so keen on shopping. At two she happily 'read' most of the major high street names on shop fronts, carrier bags and packaging just because she'd heard me say them and picked up 'clues'. (Perhaps I should have heeded the warning then and there!) But this was a useful starting point, as it wasn't long before she also picked out other common words: 'sandwiches'; 'Ladies'; 'Car Park'; 'Swimming Pool'; 'Library', 'Beach' (we live in coastal Devon) and, inevitably, 'Ice Cream'. Which, of course, candidly gives you a pretty good idea of what we spent most of our time doing together before she went to school!

On one occasion she caught out her granddad, who, knowing she wouldn't be allowed to eat ice cream before supper, walked her quickly past a shop advertising ice cream sales in words alone. But she could 'read' the word and came home protesting that Granddad had said the shop didn't sell ice cream when it *did*! She had 'read it' on the sign.

The sounds that letters and words make are a key part of the development of reading strategy – and that's where you'll hear the word *'phonics'*. Phonics simply refers to the letter sounds and blends in a word: the 'c' in crunch, for example.

> **Top Tip:** Encourage an interest in 'silly' words and rhymes – they will foster an early enjoyment of language.

'What Did You Do at School Today?'

At school, children spend time finding these 'letter blends' in a huge number of different words to see how they work, and to understand how individual words are 'built'. This helps them to make rules about the 'shape' and later the spelling of words and understand exceptions to those rules.

Children also use clues to help them 'decode' what they are reading to extract the meaning from words. At first this might mean using the pictures next to the text, but later they will be able to take clues from the *beginning* of a sentence to help them tackle the difficult words at the *end*. They may take a lucky guess at first, but with encouragement to look for clues, they gradually develop a more reliable method of decoding, to build up an ever-increasing bank of familiar words and phrases.

A BBC schools programme, *Look and Read*, which was a huge favourite with the younger children I taught, successfully applied the clues idea by using a cartoon character 'Dog Detective', complete with deer-stalker hat and magnifying glass.

Children bring books home from school almost from day one, at first for you to read to them, then to read together, and finally for them to read to you. Don't be surprised if some of these early books are wordless! Following a 'story' presented in pictures only is an important pre-reading skill, and continues to reinforce the way a story moves along once children are reading. The trick is to get your child narrating the story in his own unique way. You, too, of course – and there's always potential for a few variations!

Watching your child growing in reading confidence is one of the most rewarding things about being a parent with a

The Parentalk Guide to Primary School

child at school. As they become more confident, they'll be encouraged to read widely, both from lively reading 'schemes' – which have come a long way from Janet and John and Ladybird – and from 'real books' written by first-rate children's authors at levels to match their reading ability. They'll also be encouraged to discuss what they've been reading and how they feel about the story or how they might use the information they've gathered.

In the classroom, they'll enjoy 'shared reading' with other children and the teacher; guided reading, where a small group at a similar reading ability read together; and independent reading – curled up alone with a good book. Your memory of reading at school may very well be of 'reading to the teacher' every day, queuing up alongside her desk to do so. Teachers and assistants *do* hear children read, but the value of this exercise in the classroom is not as great as once thought. As a parent you are ideally placed to read with your child, one to one. Don't stop. One family I know continued reading to their children at bedtime – and while the children were washing up(!) – well into the children's teens, establishing a regular habit of reading and a great love of books. This undoubtedly took effort and consistency, but was worth it.

Writing and Spelling

From Foundation level children will practise writing letter shapes and by the end of Year Two will probably have begun to learn 'joined up writing'. They will work on handwriting skills every day, learning even size and spacing, the difference between lower and upper case (capital) letters, and how to write

'What Did You Do at School Today?'

neatly and clearly. More importantly they'll learn how to communicate ideas, share information and reflect on experience through their writing.

'How can I help my child with reading and writing?'

The school will give you more specific guidelines – but you could begin with the following:

- Enjoy reading at home together when you aren't rushed or tired. Sit somewhere quiet where you won't be disturbed.
- As you read, talk about the characters, the plot, what might happen next, and what happens in your own family life in connection, i.e. 'Hey, that's just what happened to Granny!'
- Praise every attempt to read a word, even if it's wrong. Find 'clues' to the word, either in the word itself or by looking at the picture, other words in the sentence, or what has gone before.
- Encourage him to read widely: signs, lists, timetables, maps and posters, as well as texts. Let him see *you* read, and involve him, whenever appropriate, in what you are reading.
- Develop the habit of using dictionaries and reference books as a family. Keep them where children can use them easily.

The Parentalk Guide to Primary School

- Encourage children to write any lists or notes (to the milkman, for instance), diaries, thankyou letters, birthday cards, postcards, stories, and little rhymes for friends and family.
- Stick words to be learnt on the fridge and have a 'word of the week' – a new, funny or interesting word you'll all try to use. Talk about the words used by newsreaders and on television and radio programmes.
- Tell – as well as read and write – 'made up' stories for each other, or take turns to tell sections of a continuing story, using a timer.
- Keep reading – and writing – to each other, throughout the primary years, and beyond.

A Note for Left-handers . . .

If your child is naturally left-handed he will not be 'forced' to write with his right hand, but may need some special help to counteract the sometimes awkward writing style left-handers develop. You can purchase left-handed pencil grips and scissors to help, and he may need to sit in a slightly different position from other children to give himself room to write, but try not to make him feel too different. Just keep an eye on his progress – there are ways the school can provide help if necessary.

Speaking

Speaking skills are an important part of language work but are often overlooked outside school. Some children arrive at school speaking only in 'soundbites' or snatched phrases and one of

'What Did You Do at School Today?'

the first tasks of an infant teacher is to teach them how to make sense through speech and to speak in whole sentences. If children haven't mastered this skill, it's unlikely that they will make an easy transition to writing or reading.

Children will also have opportunities in the classroom to explain things to each other, debate in groups, and give presentations to their classmates in the context of wider class work as well as in English. Informal speaking – legitimate or otherwise – rarely needs much encouragement!

> ***Top Tip:*** *Next time you go shopping ask your child to write the shopping list. He can try to spell some words, take 'dictation' from you for others, and find words on tins and packets.*

Spelling is learnt in much the same way as reading – by looking at patterns and phonic blends, learning rules and exceptions, and by just spending time around words through reading and writing in every form. There's a saying that spelling is 'caught, not taught' and that's at least partly true. But schools will also encourage children to develop the habit of following a step-by-step process like 'Look, (Say), Cover, Write, Check', when faced with a new word to spell.

For example:

1. **Look** at the word *'crashing'* and how it is built, and spot any 'blends' – like 'cr' and 'sh' or 'ing'.
2. **Say** the word slowly to see how it's built. (This step isn't

The Parentalk Guide to Primary School

always included as it's not always reliable – think of 'rough'!)
3. **Cover** it with your hand.
4. **Write** it from memory.
5. Go back to **check** it against the original until it's the same.

There are always exceptions to spelling rules and that's where memory comes into play – and work. Mnemonics and word rhymes will help – the sillier or more personal the better.

For example, my daughter couldn't get the hang of spelling 'necessary' until she remembered that in order not to feel sick, it might be *necessary* to '**n**ever **e**at **c**hocolate **e**ach **s**unny **S**aturday **a**fter **r**unny **y**oghurt'! It's bizarre – but it works!

Skill at recognising and using the finer points – or marks – of punctuation develops as teachers draw attention to rules and requirements while reading to a class or group. Children will gradually understand what difference punctuation makes to text as they read, and are encouraged to use it naturally as they write. They will also follow some formal written exercises both from the teacher and from textbooks or worksheets to reinforce the rules of grammar and punctuation.

Oh No, Not Maths!

Many of us still think we can't 'do' maths, yet most of us have grown into fairly competent adults who are able to budget, estimate, measure for curtains and work out mileage for a car journey. In short, we're confidently using maths every day.

'What Did You Do at School Today?'

> WE SPENT HALF OF TODAY DOING FRACTIONS, HALF DOING ENGLISH, AND THE OTHER HALF RE-DOING FRACTIONS

Much of the recent development of the Maths curriculum has been designed to remove the 'fear' of maths we may have known, to encourage creativity and problem solving, and build confidence in children as they learn. So if maths is not 'your thing', enjoy discovering just how much more fun it is for children – and join in.

A good school will run a curriculum evening to explain the Maths curriculum in an entertaining way. Resist the temptation to stay away, promising to go to the reading evening instead! Get along and get interested. Your involvement could quell those final flutters of fear and help you to help your child with confidence.

Primary Maths includes a large amount of work to develop numeracy skills. Because researchers believe that repetition and vocalising help us to remember, these skills are developed through spoken and mental maths as well as written 'sums'.

The Parentalk Guide to Primary School

You might be reassured to find that children are encouraged to learn number 'facts' (including multiplication tables) to help them calculate quickly and easily. But they will also explore shape, space and measures, and, in Key Stage Two (at around age eight) will further develop work in data handling: learning how to record, present and interpret mathematical information in graphs and charts. They will also learn a great deal through practical home projects, so there is much that you can do as a family to help. Shopping, DIY, cooking, sport and planning a journey, all use maths in a natural fun way.

> **Top Tip:** Board games and puzzles are a great way to support Maths and language work – and of course they're fun too!

Primary Science involves the children in exploring living things, physical processes and materials. They will revisit aspects of science such as Living Processes (for a study of 'Myself', and how I live, breathe, eat, etc.) in increasing complexity as they work through primary school.

Information technology, or IT, means, for the most part, working with computers: something most children enjoy. Whilst computers are used across the curriculum, IT helps children learn specific computer skills, beginning with the keyboard, word processing software and CD Roms, and working up to simple programming and CAD (computer-aided design) programmes.

'What Did You Do at School Today?'

Some schools may have a simple 'robot' that the children use to learn how to programme an object by developing a sequence of instructions.

> **'How can I help my child with Maths and Science?'**
>
> - Teach counting songs and rhymes from an early age, as well as dominoes, card and board games.
> - Involve children whenever there is counting, measuring, timing or weighing to be done. Teach them to estimate, calculate, and check and record accurately.
> - Point out anything 'mathematical' in your neighbourhood – doors numbered 2, 4, 6; shape and pattern in paving stones; the number of birds on a wire or bars on a gate; digital clocks, counters and speedos, price lists, timetables and plans.
> - Use cooking to learn about heating and freezing, bathtime to learn about sinking and floating, pets to learn about animal life, a walk in the park to observe changing seasons and light.
> - Remember that expensive equipment is not needed, just a willingness to look, listen and talk, and get involved.

The Parentalk Guide to Primary School

'What Else Will They Be Taught?'

Generally schools must spend a balanced amount of time on each subject according to its status as a *core* or *foundation* subject. (We'll come to foundation subjects in a moment.)

English and Maths, as core subjects, should be taught every day and in *Literacy Hour* and *Numeracy Hour*. (Interestingly, these 'Hours' are up to fifty-five minutes and forty-five minutes long, respectively, from Year One, increasing slightly at junior level.)

Science and Information Technology, also core subjects, will be taught for around two hours a week in total, and other subjects – known as 'foundation' subjects (confusingly not the same thing as Foundation Level work in early infant classes) – for about an hour a week. These 'foundation subjects' are 'the rest of the apple', and include History, Geography, Design Technology, Art, Music and PE.

Primary schools are quite rightly increasingly adding Citizenship and PHSE (Personal, Health and Social Education) to their foundation subjects. Citizenship introduces children – simply – to what makes society work and what their responsibility is as a member. PHSE explores elements of Healthy Living and may involve exercises in conflict management and communication – all packaged in a fun and useful way. Schools may sometimes 'block' these 'foundation' subjects together over a week or more, and include aspects of science too.

'What Did You Do at School Today?'

> ***Top Tip:*** *Your child's class teacher will usually produce a plan of work for the term covering topic areas and special projects as well as skills to be developed. Pin it up at home so that you can follow it and give support and encouragement.*

For example, in a study of 'Houses and Homes', the science element might involve testing materials through simple experiments. Design Technology will involve building a model, and Geography might consider housing needs according to climate, or cultural differences. History could involve looking at the change in housing through the ages or examining the way grandparents and great-grandparents lived. Across all subject areas children will be encouraged to look carefully, ask questions, reflect, perform key tasks and devise simple hypotheses.

This is the time to try very hard to put up with questions about anything and everything from why the world is round to whether wellington boots let in water – with experiments to test out both! You might need to slow down a bit to see the world from their viewpoint. To walk and talk and point things out to them, ask and answer questions about why, how and when things happen.

The primary school years are an ideal time to learn alongside children. The development of writing, reading and number skills means that they can now handle information in lots of new ways, yet they have not yet hit the cynical pre-adolescent

The Parentalk Guide to Primary School

and teenage years, so will still find almost anything new interesting and full of infinite possibilities! Any parent who gets involved and learns alongside their children *could* be nurturing a Nobel prize-winner, but more importantly those children will learn to enjoy history, geography and science to interpret a fascinating world – not just as schoolwork. And will have a lot of fun on the way!

> **Top Tip:** *Invest in a CD Rom encyclopaedia, and check your child safety shield for Internet access (see Further Information) so that children can effectively research on computer and Internet. Take time to do this with them and help them interpret their findings.*

A parent's role is a supporting one. So show them where to find resources and equipment, help them search the Internet and local community for information and resources, and guide them as they discuss their ideas. But don't do the work for them. I made a rule only ever to give limited 'hands on' help with something I knew my children *could* do, and *would* do easily with or without me – and always to take the lead from them. So I rolled up my sleeves to help build a huge papier-mâché map of airfields for a World War Two project. (And to carry it into school a fortnight later!) But their dad – my husband, Richard – wouldn't have written the explanation of how Bomber Command operated, neither would I have drawn the Spitfires, however much we were tempted to. That was their challenge. We would certainly offer guidance, but we wouldn't do it *for* them.

Religious Education

Each Local Education Authority (LEA) has its own unique 'agreed syllabus' for Religious Education, often dependent on the cultural background of children in the area. You can ask to see the agreed syllabus at school, and staff will tell you how it is taught. The emphasis at primary level is on personal and family experience of a faith and its impact on daily life, rather than on abstract concepts. RE is very often one of the subjects that children enjoy most at this stage – it is a stimulating and creative way for them to learn about each other.

Sex Education

The very beginnings of sex education will be introduced simply as part of a science-based 'Living Things' project at Key Stage One. But in Year Six as part of a Healthy Living project or Personal Health and Social Education (PHSE), parents are consulted about curriculum content for sex education. Most schools use well-designed video-based material with accompanying worksheets. Parents are given the opportunity to view the content before the children, so that it can be set in the context of their own family beliefs and values, and developed through discussion at home.

The Parentalk Guide to Primary School

Parents *can* choose to withdraw a child from sex education lessons – but a gentle word of warning: children who are excluded from anything at school – especially sex education or assemblies – are often isolated, and frequently do not have an easy time with classmates afterwards. Whatever they were excluded from in the classroom will very likely be passed on – in edited or elaborated form – in the playground afterwards anyway. So think carefully before excluding a child. It might be better to use this opportunity to share your values with them.

What Else?

Design and Technology is a new subject whose predecessor you might have met in the guise of woodwork or metalwork. It has known something of a transformation and now develops the skills needed to design and make things by looking at how they work, preparing, testing and reviewing designs, and learning how to improve upon them. Children (still) work with wood and metal but also with textiles and what used to be known as cookery is now 'food technology'!

PE involves Games, gymnastics and dance, including teamwork skills, movement, balance, co-ordination and ball skills. Extra-curricular sports activities and team tournaments will build on these. Later, there might be a chance to try outdoor adventure activities and all children will have the opportunity to learn to swim twenty-five metres, and develop water confidence and safety skills by the end of primary school.

'What Did You Do at School Today?'

In **Music, Art and Drama** children may meet and work with artists, actors, dancers and writers who will visit the school, and will consider the work of artists and musicians as diverse as Holbein and Hockney, Schubert and Sting. Children may not understand the complexities behind the work of artists or musicians. But they can begin to appreciate the works at their own level, perhaps by using paintings and pieces as inspiration for their own creativity and composing! They will learn about basic notation, appreciation of rhythm and structure in music, and share both personal response and ways of communicating feelings and ideas through the Arts.

Extra-curricular music lessons might be offered for a reasonable fee as part of the school day, by teachers who travel from school to school teaching small groups or individuals. Many children take this opportunity to learn an instrument in school from age seven or eight onwards. Time to dig out Uncle Stan's old tuba from the attic and buy the ear-plugs!

Ability Groups

Schools frequently choose to group children according to ability in Years Five and Six (that's ages nine to eleven approximately), as preparation for secondary school – particularly in Maths and English. This means that children are able to work with others at a similar level, and benefit from teaching which suits their learning style and pace.

If a child is struggling with schoolwork, or has particular needs, the school will work with parents to support them. Sometimes they are given a small amount of extra work for

The Parentalk Guide to Primary School

parents to help them with at home, or will join a small group with a Special Needs teacher or Learning Support Assistant or Teaching Assistant. Special educational needs are discussed in the chapter, 'As Well As Can Be Expected'.

Accidental Learning

Of course, much of what children learn at school comes packaged in anything but a conventional lesson. School assemblies, playtime, lunchtime, extra-curricular sports, and clubs all play their part. Socialising, give and take, teamwork, empathy, and self-discipline are vital building blocks in social and emotional development, and are the 'glue' of the school day.

'What Might a Typical School Day Be Like?'

Every school is different. Some schools cover Literacy and Numeracy early in the day whilst children are less tired, and may delay assemblies and less demanding tasks until the afternoon session. But imagining how your child's day might go helps to put the National Curriculum with all its confusing stages, levels, cores and foundations, in context. So here's a fairly typical day for a Year Three class – that's the first year of the junior department of primary school.

8.40–8.45 a.m. Children arrive, hang up coats, leave lunchboxes safely stored in the Lunchbox Bin and go to their tables or desks. They check last night's homework, catch up with friends, and wait for the day to begin.

'What Did You Do at School Today?'

8.55 a.m. The teacher calls the register, checks homework, and briefly explains the content of the day ahead. At the same time the children work on a short daily spelling and handwriting exercise.

9.10 a.m. Assembly – a daily event. The junior department meet in the school hall today. Sometimes children meet in year groups. A song is sung, the headteacher shares school news, and the Education Officer of a local wildlife park gives a short talk. At other times this may be given by another teacher, a charity representative, a visitor from the community or, in schools with a church link, a member of the local clergy. Children also share and celebrate each other's achievements in sport, hobbies or music.

9.30 a.m. Numeracy Hour begins. This is a compulsory Maths session. The children revise earlier work on multiplication, and as a class look again at the mechanics of multiplication with practical equipment, revising application of rules and understanding.

9.45 a.m. Time is spent in small groups, with children working with practical equipment on a range of multiplication problems. A teaching assistant sits with one group where extra help is needed. The teacher moves between groups to give guidance. At the end of about twenty minutes, each group 'reports' their findings back to the whole class. Individual work from worksheets then consolidates all that has been learnt. Children who work more quickly use extension sheets to develop their knowledge and skills. At the end of the session the teacher recaps on what has been learnt, reinforcing both the method and the mathematical language used.

The Parentalk Guide to Primary School

10.30 a.m. Breaktime. Most children play in the playground where footballs are restricted to one area, quieter games in another.

11.00 a.m. Science and PHSE. The children are working on a 'Healthy Living' project. A dietician visits to tell the children about her work, and help them discover the function of different food groups. After a short talk the children work in groups tasting a range of different foods and identifying their food value (carbohydrate, protein, vitamins, etc.). As the teacher wonders if just before lunch is the right time to do this, the children use charts and graphs to help them compile a day's healthy eating plan.

12.15 a.m. Lunchtime. The children go (quickly!) to the second sitting for lunch (infant department children go to lunch first). The remainder of the lunch 'hour' is taken up with clubs and sports activities run by teachers. Today it is the turn of Junior Netball, Recorder Group, and Environmental Club.

1.30 p.m. 'Literacy Hour'. The teacher reads from the class text – an adventure story – and draws attention to the way words – especially 'adjectives' – are used to describe action sequences.

Children spend time in groups reading a selection of excerpts from adventure stories in their 'Reading Groups', and identify 'adjectives'. One small group needing extra help works more closely with the Learning Support Assistant. The teacher spends a few moments recapping on the main points of the session and reads a short 'cliffhanger' section of the story.

2.35 p.m. PE. This is one of two PE sessions the class will have this week. Today netball and football skills are taught with a parallel class, followed by a short game of each.

'What Did You Do at School Today?'

3.25 p.m. Class time. A short time to recap on the day, remind children about homework and socialise.
3.30 p.m. Home.

... So *that's* what they do at school all day.

Bringing School Home

Nurturing a Home-School Relationship

One vastly experienced infant school head teacher sent a letter to all new parents at the beginning of the school year. It read, 'We promise not to believe all that your child says goes on at home – if you promise not to believe everything they say goes on at school!'

It's inescapable. From the day our children enter their first primary classroom, home and school will rub off on each other – and not just via the powder paint smudges carried on sweatshirts and shirt cuffs.

What goes on at school is reflected in the mood at home and what happens at home is often highlighted in the classroom. Forging links between home and school can do much to remove the blind spots which develop from a 'them' and 'us' relationship, and clarify an 'us, together' vision. But to be part of that home–school partnership and vision parents have to be prepared to get involved.

Many schools welcome the involvement of parents in every area from cake-making to policy-making, and from fundraising to after-school clubs. But some still struggle with what a 'home–school partnership' really means, and may see parental involvement as little more than occasional help in the classroom and letters home about lost property.

But if you are fortunate enough to be part of a school community that widely welcomes mums and dads, you will find that it is not only your child's experience of school that is enriched – but yours too. That said, it's important to remember that school staff do work in an environment that is always busy, often demanding and frequently stressful. The need for a home–school partnership to be one of support and co-operation is a mutual one.

Bringing School Home

Every parent will almost certainly be invited to a 'Parents' Evening' at least once a year; receive regular 'letters' and school newsletters; read a yearly report on their child's progress and be invited to join a Parent Teacher Association or Friends group. These are all excellent ways not only for you to find out what your children get up to at school, but also to begin to get to know the wider school community and find out what they might be able to contribute.

> ***Top Tip:*** *Encourage children to enter important school dates and details on your family calendar, and to check them regularly.*

'How Can I Strengthen Links Between Home and School?'

On a day-to-day basis you can make home–school links just a bit stronger by trying to:

- regularly help children with reading and homework and keeping diaries or homework notebooks up to date;
- tell the school when things are going well: 'Sarah really enjoyed the project on flight', as well as when there are problems;
- support the school's approach to discipline and reinforce it at home, or discuss sensitively with the teacher alternatives you feel might work better;

The Parentalk Guide to Primary School

- ask questions when you are confused about your child's progress or activities;
- make it a priority to attend meetings about curriculum and school policy (These are often poorly attended. Being there sends the message that you are genuinely interested in what the school is trying to do.);
- keep to school guidelines for punctuality, uniform, lunches and general organisation whenever you can – and apologise or explain when you can't;
- always telephone (or write) to the teacher if your child is going to be late, has an appointment at the dentist or doctor, or is ill;
- always ask for permission to take your child from school for other reasons.

'What Is a "Home-School Agreement"?'

Since 1999 all schools have asked parents to consider, read, and sign a 'Home–School Agreement'. (Older children might also be asked to sign, once they are able to understand the responsibility required to meet the agreement.) This simple document draws the attention of parents to points of policy – behaviour, for example – as they work out in practice what happens when Harry whacks Sally.

It will ask you to agree to certain frameworks of discipline in school, to agree to encourage your child to do homework, be on time, and behave appropriately in class. All things most parents are only too happy to 'agree' to. It is not legally binding, but it focuses the attention of parents, teacher and children

Bringing School Home

sharply on their obligations to one another as part of a partnership.

Home–school agreements are referred to if there is a problem with discipline or non-attendance, as a reminder of what you agreed to do as a member of the school community.

'What About Letters from School? Sam's Mum's Got a Letter – Where's Mine?'

Confidential letters will be sent by post, but day-to-day 'housekeeping' communications from school are often destined to turn into paper aeroplanes, trumpets and soggy lumps. The trick is to get to them before metamorphosis! Children need to be reminded to pass letters on to you, not let them fester at the bottom of their school bag to surface only after they have lost their relevance. Sometimes a 'reply slip' will have been provided, so if the letter reaches your hand late you may have missed the opportunity to make a comment about plans or policy, or for your child to take part in a special activity.

Schools are beginning to add information and updates to their school website. But not everyone has either an Internet facility or the time to check a website regularly. So although this is a bold move, soggy letter days are probably here to stay – for a while, at least. You can try to overcome the problem by:

- asking your child about letters every day to develop the habit of handing them over as soon as they get home – perhaps at the same time as an empty lunch box. But hopefully not in it!

The Parentalk Guide to Primary School

- informing the school of any change of address or telephone number so that important letters don't go astray, and you can be contacted by other means if necessary;
- remembering that *really* important news – test results, for example – will usually come home in an addressed envelope or by post;
- not *quite* believing your child's cry that, 'The school roof blew off – it's closed tomorrow!' without even a scribbled note from the teacher. If in doubt ask another parent or phone the school;
- keeping all the letters and newsletters from school in your 'school' file, so that you've got them safely to hand.

'When Should I Go into School – And When Will a "Note" Do?'

Most schools are happy for parents to call into school for various reasons, and a quick visit to the classroom for a few words before or after school is usually fine, but remember that you may be asked to make an appointment for a less busy time. It may not always be possible to see the class teacher, so you may see the head teacher, or vice versa.

> ***Top Tip:*** *Have the same friendly relationship with your child's teacher that your dentist would like you to have with her! Trust that she knows what she's doing, follow her advice, have a regular check up, and be there fast in an emergency!*

Bringing School Home

If you'd prefer to write rather than visit, a quick note is best for routine matters: 'Tom's lost his PE kit and it's not in lost property – any ideas?' will give the teacher a chance to remind Tom to look for those lost plimsolls throughout the day.

'Lucy has a hospital appointment at 11.30 tomorrow, but will be back in school for lunch' is short, to the point, and lets the teacher know when Lucy will be back in school – and consequently back within the school's sphere of responsibility.

Writing a letter can be the best way to communicate more complex enquiries or prepare the school for a later visit. It also helps you organise your thoughts clearly and gives the school time to investigate a query. Address general queries to the class teacher in the first instance, unless you are writing about a wider school matter. If this doesn't sort things out, approach the head teacher, but give her the chance to talk to the class teacher before making an appointment with you to talk things through.

Most problems are easily resolved, and are nearly always the result of a misunderstanding or simple oversight. None of us wants to turn a drama into a crisis, but neither should we hesitate to contact the school with genuine concerns. However angry or upset you feel, letters and visits should always be enquiring rather than confrontational. Ask for help and give some idea both of what you will do and what you are expecting the *school* to do in response. For example, 'Please telephone me as soon as possible with an appointment', or 'I will call in to see Miss Direct briefly after school tonight'.

If the problem is serious – an accident or incident of bullying, for instance – keep a copy of your letter, and a record of dates, times, places, and staff contacts. These details will help the

The Parentalk Guide to Primary School

school to investigate the matter more effectively and they will also document your concern. Keep them in your 'school' file and take them into school for any meetings so that you can refer to them.

School Reports

All of us will know a family joke linked to school reports. We might even be the butt of one. We cringe at that hint at future character, a dry comment or Freudian slip that 'said it all' about us – even at six and three-quarters!

Whenever I'm bossing the family around in a minor domestic drama, my husband reminds me that my school report – aged seven – told my parents that I enjoyed 'organising small groups of children into plays'. I also laugh at the 'strongly held

> I GOT ALL "B"S..
> B MORE CAREFUL,
> B EXTRA STUDIOUS,
> B BETTER BEHAVED!

Bringing School Home

opinions' he had along with 'plenty to say' at age six. Especially when I hear him bursting forth on local politics more than thirty-five years later!

Happily, school reports are now much more 'rounded' in their approach. 'Could do better' is a rare phrase, and divisive 'class positions' are rarely recorded. The teacher is interested primarily in a child's unique potential, not comparisons with others. The only time that comparisons are usefully made is after National Tests – and then the comparison is with a national average, not another child.

Primary head teachers must make a written report on a child's progress available to parents at least once in a school year. Children very often take reports home in the Easter Term, to allow for discussion and new target-setting for the following school year. Reports should include any test or assessment results, progress in all subjects, achievements in other school-based activities, and an attendance summary. Parents must also be given an opportunity to discuss the report with the child's teacher.[3]

> **Top Tip:** Don't read your child's school report as if it was the last word on their entire future.

The most useful indicators of progress will often be the general comments made by the class teacher. She gets to know the children well, and in a few sentences can give an overview of their academic progress and individual school loves and hates. But a school report is just that – 'a few sentences' – and cannot

The Parentalk Guide to Primary School

replace the value of talking with a teacher face to face.

That's why at least once a year the school will invite you to meet with your child's class teacher at the school.

'What Is Parents' Evening for?'

A regular Parents' Evening is as useful for the teacher as it is for parents. It's an opportunity to meet together more formally, look at a child's work, and learn something about both his progress and potential. Mum, Dad, teacher – and sometimes child – can set new goals together and find out more about what can be done to support and encourage each other.

Yet it's an event that many parents unnecessarily dread, almost as if they are somehow 'on trial' on behalf of their children.

I was incredibly nervous on my first Parents' Evening as a new teacher. My deputy head reassured me by explaining that if I thought *I* was nervous, I ought to see the parents. He was right. Lined up outside my classroom was a row of well-scrubbed, pink-faced Mums and Dads in their Sunday Best, anxious that their children were doing their best for the new teacher! Once I became a parent myself, I understood why!

But this really is an evening not to be missed. It's a chance to get to know your child's teacher a little better, and for her to get to know you. It's a meeting that can clarify assumptions and dispel myths without really trying.

Schools organise their Parents' Evening in various ways. Some simply arrange an appointments' system for each parent to meet briefly with the teacher. Others include a talk from the

Bringing School Home

head teacher, a school tour, refreshments – even entertainment from the children! Parents' Evening often follows on from the annual school report, as this is the ideal time to give praise where praise is due and to set targets to tackle any problem areas before the new school year.

'So How Can I Get – and Give – the Best at Parents' Evening?'
Before you go:
   Ask your child about his work and school life: What are his favourite subjects? What's difficult? What are playtimes and lunchtimes like for him? What would he change if he could?

83

The Parentalk Guide to Primary School

Are there any pieces of work he'd really like you to see? (If you can regularly update this information, and keep in touch with who his friends – and maybe his enemies – are, you will be able to enter into school-based discussions with him, and his teacher much more easily.) Then, write down any questions and concerns you may have.

Some schools allow children to attend Parents' Evening – particularly in the top years of primary school. The children hear what parents hear – comments both grumbling and great – and can be involved in target setting.

When you arrive:

Try to be punctual, arriving a little ahead of time if possible. You will probably be asked to wait with other parents outside the classroom before your appointment. Your child's work will probably be arranged here or left in his 'work tray' for you to look at. As you do, ask yourself:

- Is it generally neat, accurate and well presented when it needs to be?
- What kind of comments has the teacher made? Have they been noted and acted upon?
- Is there evidence of progress and improvement? Of interest and enthusiasm?

Also:

- Look at the work your child has mentioned that he'd like you to see.
- Spot areas where you might be able to give extra support and encouragement.

Bringing School Home

Being clear about what you want to ask will help you to make best use of the ten minutes or so you have to talk. Sometimes time slides and teachers develop a backlog of parents, so don't expect to go in bang on time. Take your child's work into the classroom with you, so that you can refer to it. The teacher will have prepared some notes so that she can make the most of her time with you. Suggest she shares these first – you might find that they answer many of your questions.

Otherwise you could ask:

- How are his friendships, behaviour and general attitude to school?
- Is he concentrating in the classroom, contributing to discussion and working well with others?
- What are his strengths and gifts? How can they be encouraged?
- How is he doing in English and Maths?
- Has he any particular difficulties? What is the teacher doing to help? How can we help at home?

If an issue crops up that will need further discussion beyond the allotted time, ask for an appointment at a later date so that you can talk in more detail. Try not to be confrontational if something you've seen or heard upsets you. Remember that both you and the teacher share the same goal: for your child to do his very best. If you become angry, it might be best to stop the conversation, and suggest another meeting soon, when you have all had time to reflect. If you feel that involving the head teacher would help, do so, but tell the class teacher, so that she doesn't feel you are going behind her back.

Hopefully though, there'll be a few pleasant surprises, one or two challenges and some fascinating – and often amusing – insights into your child's school life.

As you leave, jot down any points to remember. Take away just one or two specific targets for improvement and at least two things for which you can praise your child – no matter how hard it is!

Whether your child is with you, or waiting at home, he will usually want to talk about what was said. Try not to be angry, even if you are disappointed. Praise the positives first and if there are difficulties or weaknesses, focus on what all of you can do to improve things and suggest one or two targets to aim for. Try to end on a positive note. As mums and dads, it's important for us to avoid giving the impression that there is no hope, that school is not a good place to be, or that our children have 'let us down'. Always promise help, support, and a way through.

If you have more than one child, expect your experiences of Parents' Evening to be different with each. Our daughter always told us when things went well, but not where she was failing to put in the required effort. Consequently we always attended her Parents' Evenings with a false sense of security. Whereas our son focused on what he saw as weaknesses and kept very quiet about his strengths. His Parents' Evenings were always a wonderful surprise.

Above all make the most of Parents' Evenings. Fostering a good relationship with a child's teacher is one of the most vital things parents can do to help children succeed. A worthwhile discussion, with practical things to do as a result, will help to build that relationship.

Bringing School Home

'What About Homework?'

Homework can be a struggle at best, and a battle at worst, so it's worth thinking through some tactics to avoid outright war!

There is no doubt that children make better progress at school when academic work is a feature of home as well as school life. Most schools have a homework policy detailing how much and what kind of homework will be brought home. In Years One and Two children shouldn't bring home more than an hour a week of reading activities, spellings to learn, number work or topic-related tasks.

> **Top Tip:** Do all you can to make homework a challenge rather than a chore, right from the very beginning.

At Key Stage Two, guidelines suggest up to ninety minutes a week for Year Three and Four children, and up to thirty minutes each day for Years Five and Six. If your child brings home too much work, it could be that the work is not being completed in class, he needs extra practice or he is choosing to bring home extra work because he is anxious. Maybe he just enjoys it!

If there's less than you were expecting, he might be completing it at playtime rather than have it interrupt his evening! Or the teacher might have considered it unnecessary after a particularly hard-working day. If your child is being asked to do much more than suggested, or if work brought home falls *seriously* short, have a word with the teacher.

The Parentalk Guide to Primary School

'Why Do Children Have Homework at Such a Young Age?'

Five or six might seem very young to be doing homework. But a very small amount – perhaps just a few minutes of number work or writing – establishes good study habits from an early age, and, if it's set at the right level, the majority of children will enjoy the challenge and responsibility.

'How Can I Help?'

Most schools will send homework guidelines home, or include them in a parents' curriculum meeting. At the very least:

- Help and guide, but never do your child's homework yourself – *ever*. It's a hard habit to break.
- Check that your child is clear about what he is being asked to do, and that he has all the equipment and resources he needs.
- Don't push him – he'll just end up resenting the homework (and you).
- Find him a quiet place to work – perhaps a kitchen or dining-room table.
- Keep the TV switched off.

Younger children may need music switched off too. Some homework tasks benefit from music, others certainly suffer. Maths may be tricky accompanied by screaming rock, but reflection for creative writing can be aided by some styles of music – usually without lyrics. But music might aid concentration or provide 'company' for older children. There are no hard and fast rules. Keep an eye, or an ear, on what, and *who,* works!

Bringing School Home

At primary age few children work best shut away in their room at a desk. Most are happiest close to other activities and company, without being distracted by them. Homework is generally best done early in the evening before they become too tired to concentrate. Reading with little ones is a good activity for bedtime – but only if it's a soothing and fun activity. Most reading activities can be done curled up on the sofa anyway.

We tried to develop homework habits early, although we didn't always succeed! The first half hour or so at home from school was supposed to be 'crash out' time with a glass of milk, a snack, and TV. Then from around 5.30 p.m. was homework time, with supper at around 6.00. The children would sit at the kitchen table near me while I was preparing the meal. I was available to help; they felt warm, cosy and secure, and motivated by the sight of food getting closer all the time! They *did* moan – often – and the system did go haywire at times, but they realised this was usually the best way to get things done.

Homework Boxes

It's a good idea to keep a 'Homework Box' in a nearby cupboard. Although children will take a pencil case to and from school, a shoebox kept in an accessible place at home containing sharpened pencils, rubber, handwriting pens, a maths set, colouring pencils, sticky tape and scissors, with a 'do not remove' rule should mean they don't spend ten minutes of homework time searching for equipment. You might also like to add a good Junior School Dictionary, a calculator, some A4

The Parentalk Guide to Primary School

file paper, squared paper and scrap paper or backs of greetings cards for rough work.

'What If They Say, "I'm Not Doing My Homework!"?'

Take a moment or two to ask 'Why?' before going into overdrive! Are they too tired or anxious about the work itself? Or are they just trying to get out of it to do something more attractive? Try setting a definite time limit, or explain that the TV, video or games console can come out after homework – and *only* after. But don't get into the habit of bribing. Children have to learn that routine tasks are necessary in life and are best done before, or interleaved with, the ones we enjoy. Do your 'firm and consistent parent' bit. If homework is a real struggle, have a word with the teacher. It may be that the work is simply too hard – or even too easy.

> ***Top Tip:*** *Break homework down into a series of lumps to make it more manageable. List them with 'tick boxes' to tick triumphantly as each is completed. Allow a short break in between each one if it helps.*

Try to check their homework when it's finished, and gradually encourage them to check it themselves just before you do. Self-appraisal is a useful skill to learn. You can then draw attention to any mistakes with a 'Does that look OK to you?' and praise them for a task well done. And remember to ask how their homework was received at school. 'Did Mrs Green like your Maths?' links home and school together and reminds them that school is important – and that pride in their own efforts is, too.

'Will They Wear School Uniform?'

Your personal memory of school uniform probably includes rough grey shorts or pinafore, a frustrating tie, a hot and heavy blazer, and a sweater hand-knitted by Granny. Whilst some schools still keep to traditional uniform – very often because parents like it (in a survey in 2001, 89 per cent of parents said they preferred it!) – more have adopted an informal style of uniform and others have given it up altogether.

The Parentalk Guide to Primary School

Children can take pride in a smart uniform, but it is rarely practical, can be expensive and a burden to care for. Many primary schools have reached a practical compromise of polo shirt, sweatshirt with a school badge or logo, dark pull-on trousers or skirt, and simple PE kit. Nevertheless, whilst expense is the main reason for many primary schools dispensing with uniform, it can be a 'leveller'. Every child is dressed similarly and there will be less rivalry about labels and style. I say *less* rather than none, because even with school uniform children will still compare trainers and school bag logos!

School sweatshirts are a good way of combining identity and practicality. One local primary school in Sunderland increased the 'wearing rate' of their school sweatshirts by adding a Sunderland AFC badge to the sleeve. Innovation abounds!

Schools are also becoming increasingly sensitive to different cultural and religious needs: for example, allowing Muslim girls to wear appropriate dress and Sikh boys to wear traditional headdress.

'What About Ties?'

At primary level, ties, for most children, are thankfully a thing of the past, or make an appearance only on formal occasions. They cause frustration, serve no useful purpose (my son used to ask, 'What are they *for*?'), lengthen PE changing times, and give a bully something to grab hold of. They also get lost more easily than any other item of uniform.

When I was teaching, one of my desk drawers was named 'The Blue Snake Drawer' by the children. It was the third drawer down and opened to reveal nothing more than about twenty royal blue school ties – all 'lost property'. They lay in a curling – and the children imagined, hissing – mess. Not one of them was named (well, only as Slippery Sam or Hissing Syd) and not one of them was ever charmed – or claimed!

Which Reminds Me...

Of a conversation I had recently with a friend of mine who's a Year One teacher, and which vividly illustrates that it's often the tiny details that matter in home–school relationships.

I asked her which single thing parents could do which would make a big difference to her day. There was no hesitation: 'Name everything!' She then added, 'If you can do it, even stick a nametape on your child!'

'Teacher Says . . .'

Who's Who and What's What at School

A mother called up the stairs to her son for the third time: 'You really must get up – you'll be late for school!'

'Oh Mum!' he whined. 'Do I *have* to? The staff hate me, the kids hate me – even I hate me. Give me three good reasons why I should.'

'One,' she said, 'it's 8.15. Two, you're forty-seven years old. And three, you're the headmaster – now get out of that bed!'

If memories of staff at your own primary school include a (47-year-old) headmaster whose office door was firmly shut, and teachers who worked autonomously, you will find an enormous change in the way most primary school teaching teams work: *team* is now the operative word. As the 'captain' of the team most head teachers will aim to spend as much time as possible in a 'hands on' role within the school. They will support staff, meet parents and lead whole school events, like assemblies, Parents' Evenings or Sports Days. But they will also attend meetings outside school, with other head teachers, LEA staff, or in an advisory role in other schools or in higher education.

Much of a head teacher's job involves being an effective ambassador for the school, so much of what keeps it running day to day will be delegated to a deputy head teacher. In a large school, two senior teachers, each with specific responsibilities, might share the role.

The head teacher should ultimately give strong leadership and direction to the staff, but will delegate responsibility further to include other experienced members of staff.

Consequently, most teachers, with the exception of newly qualified teachers (NQTs), will be responsible for a specific element of the curriculum or school life. They may be in charge of Literacy development, take responsibility for a year group or school-wide concern, serve as head of year, or oversee pastoral issues.

Some responsibilities may be informally allocated, for others staff will be recruited because of their experience or specialist skills in one area. This makes for a broadly skilled team who are able to optimise and share their strengths and gifts.

Special Educational Needs Co-ordinators (SENCOs), for example, usually have specific experience, training or additional qualifications in the teaching of children with special educational needs. They not only teach children with special needs themselves, but also advise and support other staff members. A SENCO keeps track of the progress, testing and

'Teacher Says...'

referral of individual children, maintains the Special Needs Register and co-ordinates provision for children with special needs throughout the school. This includes liaison with parents and external agencies (educational psychology services, health and social services, and voluntary bodies) regarding individual children.

'How Are Primary Teachers Trained?'

The majority of teachers entering the profession will have a degree in a specific subject, for example Psychology, and an additional post-graduate qualification (PGCE) in Primary Education, or will have completed a Bachelor of Education degree (B.Ed.) in Primary Education over three or four years.

Teachers are also expected to attend regular professional development courses. These are often called INSET – In Service Education and Training. Sometimes several members of staff join the same course in a curriculum area which they feel needs attention across the school, or a subject specialist will attend a residential course to develop her interest and skills. For example, an RE specialist might attend a weekend course exploring the development of RE teaching through the Arts.

The Parentalk Guide to Primary School

IF TEACHERS ARE SO SMART, HOW COME THEY'RE THE ONLY ONES WHO HAVE A BOOK WITH ALL THE ANSWERS IN IT?

'Who Are the "Different" Teachers My Child Talks About?'

If INSET courses fall during term time or your child's teacher is absent due to illness, the class will very often be taught by a 'supply teacher', drawn from an LEA staff 'pool'. Suddenly you will hear about a new teacher who doesn't quite do things in the usual way – often at the children's outcry that 'Miss doesn't do it like that!' Supply teachers need an extraordinary ability not to be gullible!

I once had the difficult job of explaining to a young and relatively inexperienced supply teacher that the children weren't really allowed to eat their crisps and chocolate biscuits in class before break to solve the litter problem as they'd implied, but had to wait until their feet hit the playground tarmac like everyone else. She'd been had! But she learnt fast! A good supply teacher who is firm, adaptable and creative is worth the entire class's weight in gold. Increasingly, schools build a relationship locally with one or two supply teachers and employ them regularly, so that both children and staff get to know them and they become a recognised and valuable member of the school community.

> **Top Tip:** Send in an occasional 'thankyou' card to your child's class teacher, perhaps after a special project, the resolution of a problem or a school trip. Make her day!

Student teachers from university or college departments of education and school-based teacher training schemes will regularly teach children. This may be on isolated days or for a longer period of Teaching Practice. They usually bring a breath of fresh air, new ideas and enthusiasm to the school community. They are also a valuable asset and often induce hero worship from the children they teach. Visiting or advisory teachers, who specialise in a particular curriculum area, may also occasionally teach classes.

Most class teachers, especially in the early years, will be supported by at least one Teaching Assistant or TA (also called a Learning Support Assistant (LSA)). Her responsibilities will either include supporting the teacher in activities with the whole class, or specific support of one child with special needs. Sometimes she will do both across a school day. TAs usually receive at least basic training and support in their role, often have vast experience and are vital members of the school community.

The Parentalk Guide to Primary School

The Support Team

But, of course, the school team is not just the teachers and TAs. A school community would not function without an army of support staff. They include secretaries and administrative staff; a caretaker or buildings manager whose responsibility is the maintenance, safety and security of the physical school environment; cleaners, cooks, mealtime assistants ('dinner ladies'); voluntary helpers and visiting school health staff. Each one offers the children another source of adult support and friendship.

Every member of the school team is required by law to undergo a thorough professional and personal check, including a police check of past convictions, before they can begin working with children. Former employers' references and recommendations will be carefully scrutinised.

The Management Team – School Governors

All state schools and most independent schools have a managing or governing body whose responsibility is primarily to those who are 'users' of the school – the children and parents.

The number of governors will depend on the size of the school. Most primary schools have up to twelve. At least two will be parents of children who attend the school and one a teacher from the school staff.

There will also be representatives of the local authority, often – but not always – councillors or members of a local political party who have a special interest in education. Members of the local community are also co-opted and this can be especially helpful in giving a community focus to the school. Our neighbourhood pharmacist is part of the governing body of our local primary school. Her shop is right opposite the school gates and is often visited by the children and their parents, who nearly all know her by her first name. Her involvement is invaluable, as she picks up the views of parents and children naturally and informally.

Church schools include a member of the clergy or church representative as a 'foundation' governor. Whilst our local primary is not a church school, a local church minister is a co-optee and Chair of Governors. His four sons are former pupils, and he has good links with other local schools, and with charities and community organisations on a local and national level. It's this breadth of experience, perspective and enthusiasm that can transform a governing body into a creative and positive management team. Governors, when they work well together,

The Parentalk Guide to Primary School

make a positive difference to the school community. But they also have considerable powers to influence, manage and change that community.

'What Do School Governors Do?'

Some governors choose to be very 'visible' and play a varied part in the life of a school, helping out in the classroom as well as at social events. Others, perhaps because of professional commitments, will have limited involvement in the day-to-day life of the school but give solid support to evening meetings and sub-committees. Governors' responsibilities involve:

- interviewing, appointing, promoting and disciplining staff;
- deciding how many teachers and other staff the school should have;
- allocating the money given to the school by the Local Authority and ensuring it is spent wisely;
- deciding the aims and policies of the school and how it should be run;
- designing a development plan and policy documents for the school;
- drawing up and implementing an 'Action Plan' following a school OFSTED inspection.

Most governing bodies work co-operatively with the head teacher and local authority acting as a supportive, interested but critical friend. A governing body who support every proposal of the head teacher without giving it any thought or

'Teacher Says . . .'

consideration may end up inadvertently damaging the school, the education of the children and the morale of the staff, just as much as a governing body who are overbearing and interfering.

Governors meet with the head teacher in formal governors' meetings, at least once each term, and more often in subcommittees to deal with specific issues. At least once a year parents are invited to an 'open' meeting, when governors give a report on the school year, share their plans and answer any questions parents may have.

'Can I Become a School Governor?'

Parents can become more involved in the running of the school community by becoming a parent governor. It's also possible to be 'co-opted' as a representative of the local authority or community or become a 'foundation' governor as a church member, if the school has church affiliations. A desire to represent the best interests of the school and the children is the most important criterion for involvement. If you feel you want to give something back to the school community, have skills you think may be valuable – accountancy skills are highly valued, for example – or have concerns about the school that you feel should be tackled positively, ask the head teacher more about what is involved.

School governorship should never be entered into lightly. Governors carry considerable, time-consuming responsibilities and usually stay in their role for a minimum term of three years. But some governing bodies remain the same for years just because no one new wants to get involved. Schools always

The Parentalk Guide to Primary School

need fresh ideas and energy in the form of new governors – so get involved if you can.

'What Role Does the Local Education Authority Play?'

State schools are supported by the Local Authority Education Team who give advice, act as consultants and perform an administrative role. Most independent schools will have some form of relationship with their LEA. As a parent you may rarely come into contact with LEA staff. But they are busy 'behind the scenes' supporting the head teacher and governors by passing on government directives and information, and through the work of a variety of specialist staff.

The Wider Community

The more community links – like our pharmacist governor's – that are made, the more your school will be supported, and the wider community enriched. Local businesses, shops, surgeries, dentists, sports clubs, libraries and places of worship can all form useful co-operative and mutually beneficial relationships and help a community to 'own' its school.

Most schools have links with the local Road Safety, Police and Fire Service teams who make occasional visits to the children. A community police officer will also visit the school regularly and will offer advice to teachers when there are local concerns or worries about the children's safety.

The school will also have links with local secondary schools,

'Teacher Says . . .'

especially with those for whom it is a 'feeder' school, and possibly local colleges and universities too. The depth and usefulness of such relationships usually depends on the individuals or school leadership teams and often develop out of personal contact rather than policy. For example, every year for Sports Day our local primary successfully uses the wide playing fields of an independent secondary school across the road from its inner-city un-green site. It's an arrangement that fosters good relationships between two very different school communities.

'How Can I - as a Parent - Help Foster School-Community Links?'
Schools can often benefit from building relationships with the wider community.

After consultation with each other, head teacher, parents and governors together might consider:

- asking local businesses if there are ways in which they could support the school through sharing skills, donating surplus equipment or sponsoring prizes;
- making links with local sports teams to discuss how they might be able to encourage sports within the school;
- if local clubs and societies have skills they could demonstrate to the children: painting, dancing, or a presentation about local history, for example;
- asking the local health centre if a GP or Health Visitor might be able to talk to children about his or her work. Or, perhaps, visit if a classmate has a serious ongoing medical condition (such as cancer), or there is an outbreak of an

infectious illness, so that they can understand what they can do to help;
- asking a local supermarket if they might be able to help enrich classwork with a 'shop tour' or a visit from a butcher, bakery assistant or the store manager;
- whether a local residential home would benefit from visits from the children, the school choir at Christmas or a dance or drama group;
- inviting the elderly in the community into school for a musical afternoon – perhaps during a special 'World War Two Week' or at Christmas;
- inviting retired grandparents and other members of the community to offer help in teaching the children cookery, crafts, woodwork or helping them with reading;
- letting the local library know which projects each year group are working on, and asking if library events could contribute to school curriculum plans;
- finding out if there is a writer, artist, musician or TV presenter nearby who would visit the children or be 'Artist in Residence' for a day or week;
- writing to your local paper and asking them if they would include reports from the children on community life or a regular update of school news;
- contacting local tourist attractions and travel companies to ask for their help in offering special rates for the school – perhaps in return for limited promotions and advertising in the school magazine or newsletter.

'Teacher Says . . .'

'How Do Parents Help as Part of the School Team?'

Teachers, advisors, governors and support staff aren't the only adults who help the school community thrive. Parents also have a valuable role to play. Any school worth its salt will welcome the help of parents, grandparents and other volunteers, especially with reading and practical activities like cooking and artwork, and beyond the school gates for swimming lessons or school trips. Remember that if you want to volunteer regularly, you will need to go through the same screening process as other school staff.

> **Top Tip:** If you have a hobby or skill that would transfer to the classroom or you particularly enjoy sewing or painting – tell the teacher. Your strength might be her weakness – instant teamwork!

If you enjoy being with children and would like to be involved – simply ask. Don't think that you're without special skills. As a mum or dad, you will have a good idea of what makes children tick – and you might discover hidden talents along the way.

A class science project on Materials was enriched beyond expectation when the grandmother of a pupil came into my Year Six class to demonstrate spinning wool. Her skill, as well as her calm and gentle manner, completely caught the interest and imagination of the children and she joined us for several weeks to teach those who were interested individually, and to help them sort and dye the wool and weave small mats as Christmas gifts. The children would never have had such an opportunity without her enthusiasm and commitment. One of the best memories of that time – with a photograph to match – is the sight of Robbie (one of the 'liveliest' in the class) sitting, grinning at the side of a spinning wheel, unusually quiet and absorbed.

It is years since Robbie and I went our separate ways. But I like to think that somewhere in the world a six-foot-two, 28-year-old Robbie occasionally amazes his friends – and maybe even his own children – with the admission that he knows how to use a spinning wheel because Mrs Garfield taught him in Miss Knight's class when he was ten!

If you do become a classroom volunteer, stipulate the day you can help out and stick to it, so that the teacher can plan to make the most of your skills. Just turning up may prove problematic. But if you can give a morning – even an hour – once a week regularly and reliably, your help will be invaluable. Ask the teacher to give you some guidelines regarding the school day, children's behaviour and standards of work, so that you can work together effectively. Familiarise yourself with the location of equipment, toilets and other classrooms, and always abide by school and safety rules.

'Teacher Says . . .'

'How Can I Best Support My Child and His School?'

By being there for both! This relationship is a three-way one between you, your child and the school. But your support will also be communicated if you try to:

- read letters, newsletters, and any DfES parents' magazines that your child brings home, respond where necessary, and stay informed about what is happening in the life of the school;
- encourage your child to obey school rules and get to where he should be on time;
- help him with homework tasks and support topic work in the classroom by taking an interest and helping where you can;
- encourage him to look after his property by naming his belongings; help him to get organised, clean his own football boots and bring home his PE kit for washing regularly – even if it is infrequently!
- attend parents' meetings, governors' 'open' meetings, school performances, or class assemblies whenever you can;
- keep in regular informal touch with your child's teacher;
- consider being a school governor or getting involved with the PTA, and support fundraising events and initiatives;
- consider how your own gifts or professional expertise might benefit the school;
- always speak supportively of the school and its staff and

The Parentalk Guide to Primary School

channel any concerns in the right way – through the teacher, head teacher and governing body.

Do everything you can to help school be *fun*!

'How Do I Join the PTA?'

You'll normally be told about the PTA (Parent Teacher Association), PSA (Parent Staff Association) or Friends group and introduced to the chairperson at a parents' introductory meeting, and will automatically become a member when your child joins the school. PTAs are usually committee-based with some parents taking a specific role – as secretary, treasurer, or chairperson – and in turn encouraging the involvement of other parents as 'ordinary' members.

PTAs vary from school to school, both in size, activity and involvement in school life. Their energies are usually focused on school social events and fundraising, but they also provide opportunities to discuss education issues. PTAs are usually affiliated to the National Confederation of Parent Teacher Associations, which gives help, support and inspiration to member groups – you can find their details in 'Further Information'.

> ***Top Tip:*** *If your school doesn't have a PTA or equivalent, ask the head teacher why not, and consider starting one. The NCPTA have starter packs to help.*

'Teacher Says...'

The PTA will usually meet once or twice a term and at an Annual General Meeting when committee members are elected and the plan for the year ahead is discussed. Sometimes a PTA will form an informal group to arrange single fundraising events.

Whichever way a PTA is organised its purpose is to involve parents, grandparents and wider family in the school community and enrich the school life of the children, often by providing equipment and events they might otherwise not enjoy.

PTAs are also a great way to meet other parents socially. Some raise a great deal of money for their school and organise a wide range of events for parents, children and the wider community. Get involved and you could find yourself elected as treasurer, helping out once a year with a stall at the Summer

Fair, or wearing a purple sparkly wig as the DJ at a school disco! Whatever your strengths may be – go with them! And PTAs aren't restricted just to parents – grandparents and wider family can be involved too.

Other Parents, Other Children

From day one, many mums and dads discover that the most important relationships made in the context of school are those built in the playground or at the school gate, 'While-u-Wait'. The same crowd of parents and children will be gathered together in this way for six years or more – although they do go home occasionally! They greet each other each morning with everything from a polite nod to the beginnings of deep conversation, and share concerns, anxieties, celebrations and triumphs. Acquaintances often grow into life-long friendships.

Sadly it's often the playground that nurtures gossip, so it's a good idea to take all rumours about the school and its staff with more than a pinch of salt, and try to bring a positive comment into the face of every unjustified criticism. Every school playground has its band of parent critics for whom the head teacher and her team can do little right. This group may stand aloof and rarely enter the school building. They may occasionally form part of the PTA, or even the governing body. It may be your responsibility to bring some grace, stability and understanding to offset the criticism.

But even if you would prefer to kick a ball around with the children, and make your role more Manchester United than

'Teacher Says...'

United Nations you can give and gain much from the daily playground routine. And while we're on the subject of football, school is like any good team. The more you put into it, believe in it, support it and cheer it on, the better it will become.

Testing Times

The When, Where and Why of Primary School Tests

If there is a pair of words guaranteed to bring most of us out in at least a cool sweat it is 'exams' and 'tests'! Of the spiders in the bath, these two are tarantulas.

Statutory requirements for testing are perhaps the most contentious of any introduced into schools in the last twenty-five years. None of us really want them, but all of us recognise the need for some kind of measure of children's ability, potential and progress, as well as a measure of school performance. A.S. Neill, the educationalist, once said in a letter to the *Daily Telegraph:* 'If we have to have an exam at eleven, let us make it one for humour, sincerity, imagination, character –

and where is the examiner who could test such qualities?'

Most of us would agree with A. S. Neill's words. But whether we like them or not, tests are here to stay.

'When Are Children Tested at Primary School?'

Children currently face statutory testing three times during their primary school career: through a 'Baseline' test shortly after starting school and in 'End of Key Stage' tests (commonly called SATS) at the end of Years Two and Six. To us parents, it may seem ludicrous that children are exposed to testing at such a young age. But we can encourage them to view tests as another part of school life, to be taken seriously, but firmly in their stride. We need to broadcast loud and clear that, yes, academic tests are important in life – but they are not the *most* important thing. That doing well in them can offer wide opportunities and challenges in life, but that life itself can offer both without test results.

> **Top Tip:** Remember that there is no 'pass' or 'fail' in primary school tests. They are a measure, not a goal.

Baseline assessment exists to establish a starting point for children's formal learning, and Key Stage assessments find out both how far they've got and how far they might go next. They are the best estimate – tests can never be an accurate measure – to be made of how they're doing on their educational journey.

'What Are Baseline Tests?'

Children arrive in the Foundation class – on the starting blocks of primary school – with a huge variation of life experiences and skills between them. Some will have been to both playgroup and/or nursery school, others to neither. Each child's skills, and social and intellectual development will have been influenced by a variety of pre-school learning experiences, as well as by family life, hobbies, interests, personality and confidence. The aim of Baseline Tests is to discover where each child is on those starting blocks: to find out about their understanding of English and Maths, and about their level of social development as they start school. Teachers are then able to establish an accurate 'baseline' from which to measure progress, and are better equipped to offer learning activities at an appropriate level.

Parents should never feel that any preparation is needed for these tests. 'Cramming', at whatever level, does nothing to aid children's natural development, and everything to damage their self-esteem and confidence and give an inaccurate picture of their needs.

It is not a pretty sight to watch a pre-school child being 'drilled' with flashcards or expected to 'perform' all he knows for Granny or the Health Visitor, or to 'Say your letters nicely' to the plumber as he fixes the washing machine. And, yes, that dubious privilege was given to a friend of mine who's a plumber, as he fixed a washing machine outflow pipe in place! There is enough time ahead for feeling under pressure to achieve without adding to it at this early stage.

A stimulating, sociable and secure pre-school life including opportunities for talking and reading together, exploring the environment and developing early maths skills through shopping, cooking, music, rhyme and games, is the only requirement for making the best start at school – and for ensuring a realistic response to Baseline Tests. That pushy mum with the plumbing problem would have been wise to let her son watch how the washing machine was repaired. He would have learnt about water pressure rather than parent pressure!

'What Does a Baseline Test Involve?'

Baseline assessment is carried out within the first few weeks of school life, but these simple tests are so similar to other classroom tasks, it is unlikely that children will notice any difference from their other activities.

Unlike Key Stage tests, there is no one national scheme for Baseline Tests, and it is up to Local Education Authorities to recommend one of a range of tests approved by the DfES (Department for Education and Skills) to their schools. Consequently, Sam in Birmingham may be busily working on a test that is quite different to that of his cousin Lucy in Somerset.

But each test will have elements in common. It will be designed to discover what Lucy and Sam can 'do' in English and Maths, and to find out something about the development of their social skills – how they work and play alongside their classmates and teacher.

Testing Times

1. Reading and Pre-reading Skills
Can Sam manage a book properly? Does he have an understanding of the way a story has a beginning and an end? Can he recognise some key words – 'car' perhaps or 'Mummy', and his own name? Does he know the sound it begins with or the name of any individual letters?

2. Writing
Can Lucy hold a pencil properly? Can she write her own name and a few other letters? Is she able to write 'Love from Lucy' or another simple sentence?

3. Speaking and Listening
Can Sam understand simple questions and answer appropriately? Is he able to listen attentively and speak clearly to other children and adults? Can he ask relevant questions and give simple explanations – perhaps of the way a toy works?

4. Mathematics
Can Sam and Lucy count to five, ten or more and understand what they are doing as they count? Do they recognise numbers, shapes and some mathematical vocabulary like 'taller', 'longer', 'above' and 'behind'? Can they simply compare the weight and size of objects and sort them by that size, or by colour or shape? Are they able to add lower numbers together?

5. Social Development
Can Sam play well with others, taking turns, sharing and making friendships? Is Lucy able to follow instructions for a game, look after her things, and clear away?

Can Sam sit still and concentrate on tasks? Can he find his way around the school and know how to ask for help or directions?

(And, I'm tempted to add, do Lucy and Sam know how a washing machine works?!)

The results of these simple and informal assessments will help those teaching Lucy and Sam to spot gaps in the foundation knowledge and skills they need to make the best of their early years at school. They will then have a clearer understanding of what each child needs to learn next and which skills they need to develop. Teachers will continue to use Baseline results to measure what is learnt over the next two years until the Key Stage tests at the end of Year Two.

'What Are "End of Key Stage" Tests?'

These tests are commonly called 'SATS' (after their original title of 'Standard Assessment Tests'). They take place at the end of Key Stage One and Two (around ages seven and eleven) and are a good indicator, both of the progress made since the last assessment, and of what 'level' of work might be worked towards next. They are administered in Years Two and Six, so that teachers can have clear indications of appropriate expectations and goals for the junior stage of primary school (school years Three–Six) and secondary school, respectively.

The tests cover English and Mathematics at Key Stage One (KS1) at the end of Year Two and English, Mathematics and Science at Key Stage Two (KS 2) at the end of Year Six.

Testing Times

Again, there is no question of passing or failing, and only simple preparation through revision of familiar skills and practising test procedure (as these tests are more formal) is required. Most of this will be done as part of whole class preparation – with huge doses of encouragement and calm from home. Remember that spider. If *you're* anxious . . .

'How Are the Tests Given to the Children?'

There are two distinct stages to End of Key Stage Tests. Initially, the teacher assesses the children. Several key pieces of work are completed over a few days, and as the children work, the teacher will watch and listen to gain a good idea of the level of understanding and application of skills each child demonstrates in different learning situations. Teachers may take notes, but aren't allowed to help the children at this point. Then, when the work is finished, it is marked using a standardised marking scheme followed by teachers countrywide. This means that every child is assessed in the same way, and has the same chance to do well.

Once the teacher assessment has been done, children who are able will usually move on to the National Tests. These tests are presented to the children in an attractive booklet format. Key Stage One booklets have practice questions at the beginning, so that the children can familiarise themselves with the type of question before trying the real test.

Key Stage Two booklets have written instructions at the front, which explain how to tackle each question. A simple pencil icon shows the children where to write their answers and the booklet guides them through the tests page by page. At Key Stage Two there are a good mix of question styles – multiple choice, one-word answers, sentences and longer answers. These test a range of skills.

The teacher will explain all the details needed, remind the children how important it is to read the instructions carefully before they start, and will give the children some practice at working in test conditions – it's quite a skill just to sit still for a long time. Children also have to remember to work steadily and not get stuck on one question.

'What Can I Do to Help?'

First of all – try not to panic! Then prepare your child by:

- remaining relaxed about the tests yourself
- building his confidence and encouraging him to show what he knows and what he can do
- revising some keys skills little and often.

Practice and activity books are available widely in bookshops – or you may be able to obtain them through the school. They are often expensive, however, and certainly not the only, or even the best way to prepare. But they can be bright, encouraging and fun to use. They appear in a confusing array – so ask the teacher if she can suggest the most appropriate series.

- Don't put undue pressure on your child – never work when he is tired or frustrated.
- Don't expect your child to achieve above the 'level' he is working toward in class – these are tests of what has been achieved, not what might be reached by straining on tiptoe!

Testing Times

End of Key Stage Tests take place each May – so don't plan an annual holiday for that time if a child is in Year Two or Six.

Teachers, for their part, will try to make the experience of tests as 'special' as possible, so that the children can treat the tests both as a serious challenge and as an opportunity to show just how well they can do. It's a careful balancing act – but you can help by supporting this approach at home.

> ***Top Tip:*** *Cook a favourite meal or arrange a treat for after the tests to help them relax and forget about it all. They've done their best – and that's the thing to celebrate!*

The Parentalk Guide to Primary School

The results of End of Key Stage Tests will usually be sent home with your child's end of year report and will appear as 'levels'. The school may produce a leaflet to explain what the results mean. Remember that each 'level' reflects a wide range of ability. Children might just scrape into Level Three, or have demonstrated skills and understanding at the very top of the level, but will both still be at 'Level Three'.

Children whose first language is not English, and children with special educational needs will almost always score at a low level. But try not to worry. The school will use each set of results to ensure progress is maintained and needs are met at *every* level for every child.

You'll always have the opportunity to discuss the results with the teacher, but think carefully before sharing them with other parents. Remember that the results are not a prophecy of a child's future life or a prediction of his anticipated educational achievement. He could just have had a 'bad' day – or, we hope, a 'good' day. If the results are not as good as you'd hoped, try not to be angry or disappointed in front of your child. Think about what you can do to see him do his very best – despite this single piece of paper with 'levels' on it.

Other Tests

Schools may use other tests produced by the Qualifications and Curriculum Authority at the end of other school years. They are optional, and not all schools use them, but they are useful for keeping an extra check on progress.

'Reading Age' tests may be used to monitor children's reading

Testing Times

development, and verbal reasoning tests may be given to some children towards the end of their time at primary school – especially if they are considering taking selection tests for secondary school.

'What Are Selection Tests?'

When children reach Year Six at primary school, they and their parents are required to make decisions about a choice of secondary school. That choice may need to be made earlier where a LEA maintains the grammar school system, or if a child is at an independent school.

Most independent secondary schools, state grammar schools and some independent preparatory schools (for children aged nine to thirteen years) will ask children to sit selection tests before considering their admission.

These tests are generally a mixture of verbal and non-verbal reasoning tests, with papers in Maths and English and specialist or supplementary subjects. The school will give parents details of the kind of preparation needed to help children do their best. The chapter 'Eleven Plus' considers selective tests and their implications in more detail.

> **Top Tip:** *Your child is unique – both you, and he, need never to forget that – whatever the test results say.*

The Parentalk Guide to Primary School

Testing the School – Inspections

The purpose of End of Key Stage Tests has always been to test the *school's* ability to give your child the educational provision he needs, and to test his ability against other children to monitor national standards. Teachers will review test results, consider where expectations have not been met and where they have been exceeded. They will then work out the implications for future teaching plans and objectives. But schools also need a broader method of assessing performance over and above just the achievements of children in tests.

That's where OFSTED comes in. And come in it must!

All schools in England and Wales (Scotland has its own inspection body) will have been inspected at least once in the last four to six years by inspectors from the Office of Standards in Education (OFSTED). The aim of inspections is to improve schools, to make sure schools are doing their job effectively, and that adequate teaching standards are being reached.

'What Do I Do When My Child's School Is Inspected?'

If a school faces an inspection by OFSTED, parents will be informed about six weeks in advance. Just before the inspection, you will be sent a questionnaire to fill in with details of your experience of the school. You do not have to put your name on the questionnaire, and the school will not see it before the inspectors. The papers are returned to school in a sealed envelope. This means you will be able to be fair but honest about your own experience and that of your child. You will be asked general questions like 'Does your child enjoy school?',

Testing Times

'Are you satisfied with the amount of homework your child is given?', 'Do the staff listen to your questions and queries?'

You will also be invited to a confidential meeting for parents, to which staff will not be invited, unless they have their own children at the school. (Understandably, you will not be able to name or criticise teachers individually at this meeting.) This is an opportunity to raise concerns, but also to highlight those things the school does well.

Inspectors will be in school for about a week, and the atmosphere may be tense.

Be aware that teachers will be busier than usual and try to be understanding of their feelings. It's often the very best and conscientious teachers who worry most about an inspection.

'What Do Inspectors Do?'

The inspection team literally look at everything and talk to everyone to give themselves as full a picture as possible of the school community and how it is working. They will talk to parents, children, support staff and teachers. They will look at the way the children work, how enthusiastic they are, the materials they are using and even the state of the chairs they are sitting on. They will want to assess the progress of pupils, the performance of teachers, the leadership of the head teacher and the oversight of the governors.

> **Top Tip:** *Support the school and the teachers as they prepare for the inspection visit by carrying on as normally as possible. If you usually visit the school as a volunteer, ask the staff beforehand how you can best help.*

What Happens Afterwards?

The inspectors will produce first a summary report and then a full report of their findings. Every family with a child at the school will be sent a copy of the summary report, and parents can ask to see the full report at school, or obtain a copy for a small cost. The report will cover a wide range of subjects, from what the school does well to the quality of teaching. It will also tell parents how the school has improved since its last inspection.

Once the school has received the report and parents, staff and governors have seen it, the school will be given five weeks to write an 'Action Plan' based on OFSTED's findings. This should demonstrate how the school plans to tackle areas that need improvement. Governors will send a copy to parents and update them on the progress in reaching those targets in their Annual Report at an open governors' meeting. Even if the school receives a glowing OFSTED report, there will always be things that can be worked on and made even better.

In the rare event of inspectors finding what they call 'significant weaknesses' the school will be given extra help, perhaps

Testing Times

through a change of staff, to strengthen those weaknesses and get the school back on track. Everyone – including parents – will have to work extremely hard to make that happen. But it can be done.

Use your own judgment to decide – against a background of personal experience – whether the weaknesses are serious or the criticisms fair, and look at whether your own child is thriving.

Your child's happiness, security and education must never be needlessly sacrificed. But this may be the time to really get behind the school, not to desert what is seen rightly or wrongly as a sinking ship. Help all you can and you could make a real difference to the school, the staff, individual children and the wider community. Ask the head teacher what she plans to do to see improvements and offer your support – you may both be reassured.

> ***Top Tip:*** *Don't automatically feel that you should move your child if his school gets a weak OFSTED report. Sometimes a move can cause more problems than it solves.*

'What Are "League Tables"?'

School Performance Tables, or so-called 'League Tables', are compiled for primary schools on the basis of End of Key Stage (SATS) tests.

If children in the school score highly in these tests, the listed results will obviously reflect well on the school. But the Tables are open to an enormous amount of criticism, and you don't have to be in a school at the top to work out why! Schools in areas where there are marked social problems or generally less family commitment to education as a priority, will almost certainly be at a disadvantage compared to schools in wealthy middle-class areas where families and schools are well motivated and mutually supportive.

The greatest critics of School Performance Tables are very often the head teachers themselves. Surprisingly, though, it tends not to be those in charge of schools further *down* the tables who criticise, but those leading the more privileged institutions at the top. They recognise the pressures and constraints placed on colleagues and pupils in challenging schools, and acknowledge the unbalanced picture League Tables can give of their hard work and professionalism.

> ***Top Tip:*** *Read School Performance Tables with local knowledge, personal experience and a healthy degree of scepticism. General guides they may be, prophecies of the school's commitment to individual children they are not.*

Testing Times

Pressure – The Plumber's Mate Returns?

Whenever children, staff, or even parents are put under scrutiny, tested, or asked to give an account of themselves, their self-worth and security is threatened. Sometimes it's all too easy to stand in the playground – or the kitchen – and play the game of 'My child one-upmanship' in an attempt to make ourselves feel better, to redeem our child's poor performance, or to save face in front of friends and relatives. If only we could all stop playing the game we might be able to better support one another.

Of course, each of us is proud of our child. Of course, we want them to do well. But we may have to ask ourselves regularly if we want them to do well because it is good for them – or because it reflects well on us? Are we expecting so much of them that their fundamental sense of self-worth is threatened? Are we in danger of loving them for what they do, or what they might achieve, rather than for who they are? What messages are we sending to our children about what really matters to us?

Julia, as the representative of a local children's charity, recently began a term of office as a governor at a special school for children with a range of learning difficulties and special needs. One of her first duties was attending the school prize-giving. As she was busy, she didn't give much thought to it beforehand, and admitted that in the back of her mind she carried a picture only of the prize-giving at the grammar school her two daughters attend – high grades, high expectation, high flying.

Nothing, she said, could have prepared her for the emotional impact of that very special morning. There were no prizes for ten A*s, for outstanding intellectual ability or giftedness. Here, one small boy received a 'King of the Cloakroom' prize because he had managed to learn – over a process of many months – to take off his coat and hang it on a peg, change his shoes and hang up his shoe bag leaving everything tidy. Another had finally learnt to write her name and those of her family, and say them, at age eleven. A third was praised for just managing to make it into the classroom each morning without losing control and running back, hysterical, to the safety of his mother's arms.

Julia said she had never cheered so loudly or clapped so hard before. Nor had she seen such glowing pride on the faces of children and parents alike or noticed such a total lack of competition. She spent much of her time looking for a tissue to dab her eyes. I have a hunch that A.S. Neill would have loved to be there with her.

Let's keep life – and tests – in perspective.

'The Best Days of Our Lives'?

What to Do When There's a Problem

'The best days of our lives.' It's a phrase that conjures up a nostalgic mix of the Bash Street kids, *St Trinian's* and *Goodbye Mr Chips*. Yet for some of us, our schooldays were anything but the best years. We may still feel the humiliation they brought, hear the negative words of a teacher echo across the years, or continue to wince at the stings inflicted by fellow pupils. We may even struggle to break free from the low expectations and self-esteem which have clung to us ever since.

My own children had their share of fraught Fridays and miserable Monday mornings.

One day when everything seemed to have gone wrong for my son, then aged about nine, and he knew he had to face the

The Parentalk Guide to Primary School

difficulties the next day would bring, he said, 'Oh, tomorrow, I could screw it all up and throw it in the bin!'

So, what can parents do, when things go wrong and tomorrow belongs in the bin?

Of course, every day has its ups and downs, and part of growing up is learning to cope with the disappointments and frustrations of life, in and out of school. But if parents have real concerns about their children at school, it's important to take those concerns to the class teacher or head teacher as soon as they arise. If the problem is serious, for example, if we suspect a child is being bullied, if there is an accident in school or a child's work is suffering because of specific anxiety it's important to monitor the situation carefully, and keep a note of dates, events and conversations with staff.

'The Best Days of Our Lives'?

Usually we can support our children with little more than love and encouragement. But very occasionally the situation may become so serious that a complaint against the school or a member of staff will be necessary. If it comes to involving the governors at this point or even writing to the Local Education Authority, parents must be able to present a clear case and not forget those important details, however minute.

Our society is an increasingly litigious one, and we cannot lay the blame for every bump and dent of school life at the head teacher's door. But neither can we ignore the risks our children face. There has to be balance in the way we seek to guide and protect them.

'What Happens If My Child Is Behaving Badly?'

Most children have days when their behaviour goes off the rails for understandable reasons. But if a child has severe behaviour problems, parents may be asked to meet the teacher or head teacher to try to sort the problem out. Very often two or three wise heads bent together can discover why a child is behaving in a certain way and work out tactics to change things for the better. Even when there are problems with a child at home, the teacher might be able to shed some light on the situation.

If the problem is with another child, it's often wise to mention the situation to the teacher first. Avoid the temptation, however strong, to confront another parent directly. However protective and angry we might feel, fisticuffs at twenty paces in the playground is not the best example for our children! Consultation is better than confrontation.

The Parentalk Guide to Primary School

Every good school will have a discipline or behavioural guidance policy, which should be followed closely. Children need boundaries for their behaviour, and that need multiplies in a school environment. Teachers look for the support of parents in implementing discipline policy and parents may receive a copy of the behaviour and discipline policy to read and/or sign as part of a home–school agreement.

> **Top Tip:** If there's a problem, view it as something that you and the school can sort out together. Not as something that will drive you apart.

Schools employ a variety of methods to enforce boundaries of behaviour. 'Time Out' is widely used. A child may be given two or three warnings about behaviour and then excluded from the classroom. Other options may include being sent to the head teacher, or told to work in a 'neutral' area where several members of staff can supervise him. At the first primary school at which I taught, children were sent to stand outside the head teacher's door. This meant that he would frequently open the door to find a quaking child outside waiting for his wrath.

Robbie – whom I've already mentioned as one of the liveliest and most challenging boys in the school – could also be great fun! We just had trouble making him understand when this particular brand of 'fun' was unacceptable! One day Robbie admitted to me that on one occasion, when I had finally despaired and sent him to 'the spot', the headmaster had duly appeared from behind his door and asked him what he had done. Robbie merely nodded towards the barometer on the opposite wall and

'The Best Days of Our Lives'?

said, 'Nothing Sir – I've been sent to take the readings on the barometer. It's a stormy day, isn't it, sir?' This was said with a nod towards the wild, inclement Cornish weather seen whipping up the waves in the distance. The head teacher told me later that he hadn't known whether to punish Robbie's cheek or praise his ingenuity. Every form of discipline has its loopholes!

I THOUGHT I TOLD YOU TO GO TO THE END OF THE QUEUE?

I DID, TEACHER – BUT THERE WAS ALREADY SOMEONE THERE

But if a behaviour problem is serious the class teacher or head teacher will discuss with parents what measures they wish to take, and what mutual support can be given.

If this happens to you, try not to take it as a criticism of your parenting. Like you, staff will genuinely want to find out what the problem is and work towards a happy improvement.

Stealing

In the first few months of school, there can often be a lot of confusion about rights of ownership. Some children genuinely won't understand that equipment, toys and games belong to school and can't become their own. At other times children will see no reason why they can't help themselves to the toys and equipment belonging to other pupils. Many children take small items from others. Sometimes they do it to have, and feel, the same as a child who's popular, or they may give the stolen object to someone they want to impress.

If a child has been clearly taught at home that stealing is wrong, they can feel powerless in the face of what they see as flagrant disobedience of the rules. In his first term at school my son saw another child take a 'transformer' figure from the tray of another boy during break, and, horrified, said to him, 'That isn't yours, you mustn't take it.' The other boy simply said, 'I want it.' And walked away. After school my son reported the incident to me with wide eyes and great emphasis, 'But Mummy – that's stealing, and stealing is *wrong*.'

> ***Top Tip:*** *Share your values with your child – or they might pick up those values you'd rather they left behind.*

It can be hard for children to come to terms with the wrongdoing of others and to deal with disappointment when things aren't 'fair'. But life isn't 'fair', and parents may often need to make the most of these incidental opportunities and conversations to pass on and reinforce values, which will help to counteract their child's disappointment.

'The Best Days of Our Lives'?

Pastoral Care and Mentoring Schemes

Most schools will assign one teacher to be responsible for pastoral care, and informal counselling. She may also have oversight of pupil mentoring schemes. These schemes usually involve older children, and give them the opportunity to draw alongside younger ones who are struggling, perhaps with bullying, or with social isolation. Mentors usually receive some simple training in communication skills and pastoral care, and will then act as a point of contact for other children, under the supervision of the teacher. Children often find it easier to share problems with their peers than with a teacher – although the pupil mentor will be given guidelines as to when confidences are best shared with an adult. Most simple problems can be resolved responsibly without the intervention of staff. Such positive outcomes benefit all the children in terms of confidence and independence.

'What If My Child Doesn't Want to Go to School?'

At some point in a child's school career most parents will have early morning conversations with a talking duvet – a reluctant schoolchild in disguise. They will go something like this:

Parent: 'Come on, it's 7.30!'
Duvet: 'I'm not going!'
Parent: 'There's no "not" about it – everyone has to go to school.'
Duvet: 'Well, why don't you go then?'

Of course, it's not usually school in general that's the problem, but an incident on the horizon, a difficulty with work or a fall out with friends or a teacher. A chat on the edge of the bed or over breakfast, a promise to send a note into school or take some other action will often be enough to set things right. But habits of 'OK, don't go in today then' or 'Just this once' are easily formed but much more difficult to break. The monster of today has a habit of doubling in size by tomorrow.

Children have to learn that school is a non-negotiable. They may have to endure bad days and you may have to arrange meetings with the teacher to make things easier or to get to the root of the problem, but it is generally true that 'everyone has

'The Best Days of Our Lives'?

to go to school'. We are not doing our children any favours in preparing them for adult life if we start 'letting them off' at age seven – or at 7.00 a.m.

You may often have to be firm, occasionally furious – sometimes even fabulously funny – but get him into school you must. And sometimes you will probably have to take him there.

If a child is reluctant to attend school or plays truant at any time it will probably be the head teacher or head of pastoral care who will liaise with parents to find out what's going wrong. Parents are legally obliged to ensure that their children attend school – and developing good attendance habits from day one is important. Not just for school – but for life.

It's not appropriate to take children out of school for a day to go shopping, visit a relative, or because we are too busy to take them. Illness, family bereavement, trauma and medical care are usually the only legitimate reasons for missing school. Days off for holidays or special events require the permission of the head teacher and the completion of an authorised absence or 'holiday form'.

A child's school report is required to give details of attendance, including 'non-authorised' absence – those days when parental permission was not given for a child to be absent, but he was not in the classroom. If truancy or non-attendance persists, the school is obliged to inform the Local Education Authority. It's at this point that School Welfare officers will become involved.

Bullying

Cast your mind back to your primary school playground. You may not be able to remember the colour of the classroom door, or the faces of the dinner ladies, but doubtless you can remember the name of the school bully. Perhaps you encountered more than one in your time at school. Or maybe *you* were the bully – or the one most severely bullied.

Bullying is as old as the abacus we learnt to count on. As long as there have been victims there have been bullies. What's more, bullying is hard to define or prove, and whilst its group nature means it is rare in infant schools, it happens with increasing frequency, and often peaks at the top of the junior school. Bullies often genuinely believe they are doing no such thing, and what one child may brush off as 'life – and just kids' will terrify another. But because bullying is potentially so very serious – we've all heard of children who have resorted to harming themselves, or others, as a result – it must never be dismissed.

Bullying needn't be physical violence. It can be verbal attack or silent intimidation.

When there is violence it can be against property – including schoolwork – or person. What makes it so painfully absorbing for the one being bullied is the fact that the fear of threats is as great as the bullying itself. A negative relationship is formed between victim and bullies, which perpetuates the isolation and fear of the victim – and the power of the bully. What distinguishes bullying from isolated acts of aggression or violence is that it is almost always done by a group, and at the insistence

'The Best Days of Our Lives'?

of a ringleader. The group may even contain former friends of the victim, or former victims of the ringleader who have 'signed up' to save their own skin.

It is hard to say why children bully, as the reasons are not always obvious, and it's not always helpful. It's true that children can be bullied because they're different, have freckles, or are slow, but they can also be bullied because they are bright, gifted or pretty – or just because they are there. Finding out 'why' doesn't stop the bullying anyway, and stopping it should be the priority. Get it stopped first – and worry about why it happened later.

The one thing all victims will have in common is the belief – their own and that of the bully – that they are powerless to stop what is happening. It's this sense that there is no way out that can push children to the very edge.

> **Top Tip:** Always take children's reports of bullying seriously – never try to trivialise an incident or laugh it off.

Every school encounters bullying in some form from time to time. It is insidious, and often so subtle that it is difficult to spot or prove. But careful management of incidences of bullying can make it the exception rather than the rule. The smallest incident should always be treated seriously in an attempt to 'nip it in the bud' according to a carefully thought-out anti-bullying policy which empowers the victim and shows zero tolerance to the bully. Every school must send the message loud

The Parentalk Guide to Primary School

and clear that bullying of any form will not be tolerated. But of course – that's easier said than done.

'What Should Schools Do About Bullying?'

First, schools have to admit that there will always be a bullying problem, always believe victims and always follow their bullying policy. Both bully and victim need to know what the response to any bullying will be. More importantly the victim needs to know that there *is* a way out.

It is crucial that any response includes some kind of mechanism for making bullies face up to the consequences of their behaviour. They need to *really* know what it is they are doing. Certainly the most hopeful policies do seem to be those where a process of skilled and systematic counselling or structured and regular discussion insists that the bully confronts the consequences of his actions. Bullies often genuinely do not realise the harm they are doing. 'It's only a bit of fun!' they say. 'We didn't mean to hurt him.'

Bullies have to understand that it was not fun – and certainly did hurt the victim. It is not enough for a child to be told to walk away, ignore it, fight back or 'Stick up for yourself!' It is the bully and the bullying that have to change, rarely the victim.

Neither is it enough to lecture the bully, give pep talks about being kind to each other, or make a public spectacle of him – that's often a kind of glory in itself. Bullying is active and leaves an impression – the school's response needs to be and do the same, but *positively*.

'The Best Days of Our Lives'?

'How Will I Know My Child Is Being Bullied?'
Possible signs include:

- reluctance to go to school;
- going to and fro by a different or longer route;
- arriving home late or leaving late to avoid the bullies in waiting;
- money, clothes or equipment missing or broken;
- extra requests being made for money, sweets or toys (to give to the bullies on demand);
- lack of enthusiasm at home, a drop in self-esteem or depression;
- imaginary or genuine sickness, headaches, bedwetting or 'tummy pains';
- frequent or sudden loss of friendships.

All of these can occur for other reasons than just bullying – but you will know your child best and have some idea of how he normally reacts to stressful situations. And don't always think, 'My child tells me everything.' However close a relationship you have, he may choose not to worry you, or feel it is important to sort this out himself – especially if he feels you have other worries.

My daughter was bullied during two separate terms at junior school – with very different outcomes. The first time she told me we acted fast. We met with the teacher and got things sorted. In fact, she even won a 'Supermum' prize for me in a national magazine with the letter she wrote about how we tackled it together. Despite this, as the second pattern of bullying incidents began she kept them to herself, feeling that she should now be

The Parentalk Guide to Primary School

able to cope. The whole pattern lasted a full term, but it was three *years* before she tearfully told me what had happened and how difficult it had been. She admitted that I had often asked her if everything was OK. I had noticed that something was wrong, but she still felt she couldn't tell me.

My son, in turn, philosophically dealt with a less serious situation by saying he just had to get through it because, 'Life is horrible sometimes.' Bullying, its consequences and its aftermath, is not as straightforward as we often believe. There are no easy answers. Adults can help by remaining alert, being ready to listen, and being there for the children. Home can provide a safe refuge where they can feel valued, loved and understood in the hope that security, confidence and self-worth will help them cope, because 'life *is* horrible sometimes'.

'The Best Days of Our Lives'?

> **Top Tip:** Don't dismiss too easily the possibility that it could be your child who's the bully.

'What If It's My Child Doing the Bullying?'

Not all bullies are big and menacing with a slingshot in their trouser pocket. Bullies can be clever, popular, attractive and bully for no particular reason other than for something to do or for 'fun'. Parents are right to be concerned if a child's friendship groups often change or he suddenly talks maliciously about a child he was formerly friendly with, admiringly of others about whom little was heard before, or boasts about daring deeds.

If you discover that your child is bullying, you can make a huge difference both to the immediate situation, and to how bullying is handled in the school, by supporting the school, the victim, and your child as you help him confront his actions and their consequences. Begin by talking to him calmly but firmly. Try to get him to explain how the bullying came about, but also make it clear that bullying is not acceptable for any reason. Then talk to his teacher. It may not be easy to make such an admission, or to have your fears confirmed. But it's much worse being the victim.

> **Top Tip:** Be very wary of a school that says, 'We never see bullying here!' – they're probably not looking hard enough!

The Parentalk Guide to Primary School

Children very often develop their own tactics for coping with 'the big boys'. When my son was about seven, on walking through the park after school we passed two boys who I knew didn't have the greatest reputation for love and tenderness where other children were concerned. As they passed my son they gave him the thumbs up and said, in friendly tone, 'Alright, mate?' He returned the thumbs up and the 'alright' and we walked on.

Intrigued, I asked, 'Friends of yours, love?' To which he replied, 'Well, Mum, they're not friends and they're not enemies.'

Wise move, I thought.

School Activities

Every so often the media highlights a tragic school accident, that has usually occurred on a school trip. It's a moment when every parent thinks, 'That could have been *my* child.' We experienced that sense several years ago when, in what became known as 'The Lyme Bay Tragedy', a group of teenagers from a local school lost their lives on a canoeing holiday in Dorset.

It somehow seems so much more disturbing for children to be injured or killed at a time when they are supposed to be having fun, or making the most of wider opportunities.

'The Best Days of Our Lives'?

'So Who Is Responsible for Our Children's Safety When They Are at School or Enjoying School Activities?'

Children remain the responsibility of the school staff at all times within school hours, whether they are in the school building, playing hopscotch on the playground or (with parents' consent) enjoying educational visits, sports matches and activity trips.

Many schools have responded to increased security concerns by implementing 'visitor' procedures, security systems, CCTV and entry cards in an attempt to safeguard the children whilst on school premises. But attacks on children in school are mercifully rare. More accidents occur during everyday school activities and trips away, although we have to remember that many more children are injured while in the care of parents or other adults than while under the care of teachers.

Parents are always asked to sign a consent form whenever their child leaves the school premises – whether for an afternoon walk to the local museum, a day trip or an activity week. This form will give consent for the teacher in charge to seek medical treatment should it be necessary, and hands the responsibility for that child to the group leader.

Ruth teaches a Year Two class and says she vividly and daily lives with the fear of an accident happening to a child in her care. Such responsibility is not taken lightly.

Recent legislation does now govern the running of out-of-school activity centres used by schools for educational trips. One of the positive outcomes of the Lyme Bay tragedy was the overhaul and efficient regulation of outdoor pursuit centres and the compulsory training of those who run courses. There are also extensive guidelines and training programmes for teachers who have a key responsibility for outdoor activities

The Parentalk Guide to Primary School

and events, a role that is often assigned to the head of PE at a primary school.

Teachers follow guidelines laid down both by their Local Education Authority and in the DfES *Handbook for Group Leaders*, which contains good practice, health and safety rules and standards for overseeing educational visits – it is often used by LEAs as a basis for their own guidelines. The purpose of the handbook is to provide practical information that might be helpful to group leaders and others, day to day, whilst taking part in an educational visit. It includes advice on supervision, ongoing risk assessment, emergency procedures, and some specific types of visit, and is updated regularly on the Internet at www.teachernet.gov.uk/visits.

> ***Top Tip:*** *If you are unsure about the supervision on a school expedition, ask questions until you get satisfactory answers. Your questions might just expose a weakness that can be addressed.*

Generally, the group leader, or senior teacher, has overall responsibility for the group at all times and follows strict DfES guidelines for adult/child ratio and corresponding safety procedures when delegating that responsibility to other adults.

What If It All Goes Wrong?

If your child has an accident, you are concerned about the behaviour of a member of staff towards him, or you want to

'The Best Days of Our Lives'?

make a formal complaint about the school, its facilities or a member of staff, always talk to the head teacher first. Try to give her some idea of the nature of your enquiry so that she can find out some background information before meeting you.

If you feel you haven't been heard by the head teacher, or are not satisfied by the response you've received, you can approach the governors and, finally, the Local Education Authority.

Happily, the vast majority of parents will have little reason to approach the school with complaints, or to worry unduly about their child's safety. If a school is made up of individuals who communicate effectively, who genuinely care for their school community and who have the best interests of the children at heart, parents can have confidence in its ability to give children, perhaps not *the* best but certainly *some* of the best days of their lives.

'As Well as Can Be Expected'

Special Educational and Medical Needs

This chapter is all about the special educational needs some children may have, and what primary schools can do to meet them. It's also to let you know what primary schools should do in response to the health and medical needs of the children in its care – and highlights one or two of the itchy problems children might encounter along the way!

For most children, primary school will be a happy mix of challenge, fun and achievement. They will rarely encounter serious problems or struggle unduly with academic work or the demands of a school environment. But for children with special educational or medical needs and their parents, school can be more about challenge than conventional achievement.

If a GP or Health Visitor identifies a special educational need in regular pre-school checks, support will be offered through child health and social services. Parents can also contact an appropriate local voluntary organisation or national charity for advice. Children who have a 'severe learning difficulty' (SLD) that is evident from pre-school age, will receive special help throughout their school life.

Wherever possible, children with special educational needs will be educated in a mainstream primary school, with the support of a Teaching (or Learning Support) Assistant, and with further support from other agencies at the discretion of the Local Education Authority. Special educational needs have a legal definition which is broad and practical: 'Children with special educational needs all have learning difficulties or disabilities that make it harder for them to learn than most children of the same age' (quoted from the Special Educational Needs Code of Practice, see p. 158). This does not include children whose difficulties stem from not having English as a first language – although they may need special education for other reasons.

Generally, children with special educational needs may need extra help because they have difficulties with the development of:

- thinking and understanding;
- physical or sensory skills;
- speech and language skills.

Or because they have:

- emotional or behavioural difficulties; or
- relational and social difficulties.

'As Well as Can Be Expected'

Some children will have special educational needs for a short time in their school career, others for much longer.

'What Do I Do If I Am Concerned about My Child?'

It can be devastating for parents to realise that something is 'wrong' with their child – medically or otherwise. We all want the very best for our children, and to see them fulfil their potential in every way. You are bound to feel upset, bewildered, to ask why, even to feel guilty and want to blame yourself, someone else or a particular set of circumstances or experiences.

The important thing to remember is that he is still the same child, that he remains unique, and that he needs you to fight his corner and cheer him on – now more than ever. Try not to think too far ahead, to make dramatic pronouncements about what the current situation might mean, or dwell on the negatives. Get help.

If learning difficulties develop once your child is at school, or you are worried that he is having problems which the school doesn't seem to have identified, get advice straight away. Talk to the class teacher, the SENCO (Special Educational Needs Co-ordinator) or the head teacher. Share your concerns and get their perspective. Working alongside the teacher will often sort out minor problems.

The Parentalk Guide to Primary School

> **Top Tip:** *Remember, you know your child better than anyone else, so if you are concerned that he may have a learning difficulty, ask questions – and keep on asking.*

A specific or general learning problem might begin on school day one or four hundred and one. It could be recognised because of a child's inappropriate behaviour or through a difficulty with reading, hearing or understanding.

It's often parents who have difficulty convincing the teacher that there's something not quite right – not the other way round. Often there will just be niggles to begin with. A sense that something isn't quite right. You may decide just to monitor the situation and see how things go. It may just be a hiccup in development or behaviour, or it may be some time before the full picture can be pieced together.

Anna and Mike were concerned about Anthony before school, although his Health Visitor assured them that he was just a quiet and slightly 'unusual' boy. But when Anthony started school at four years old, his problems were exacerbated. He found it increasingly difficult to relate to other children, to follow instructions or to deal with any disruption to his routine. Anna said, 'We endured several months of heartbreaking dialogue with his class teacher and head teacher who simply felt he was a "naughty boy" who was determined to be awkward and disruptive. They said we were "making up" our claims that there was something wrong to excuse his behaviour.'

Yet Anthony was warm and affectionate at home and,

'As Well as Can Be Expected'

although the same difficulties were exhibited there to a lesser degree, Anna and Mike felt that school was the problem. 'In the end,' says Anna, 'I was just beginning to have my own suspicions about whether Anthony might have Aspergers syndrome – a mild form of autism – when a student teacher on Teaching Practice in Anthony's class, with a special interest in special educational needs, asked me if we'd ever considered this might be Anthony's problem.

'From then on the pieces just fitted into place. It was such a relief. I read everything I could lay my hands on, we saw a paediatrician at the local Child Development Unit and Anthony eventually received the support he needed.' Anthony now works with his LSA, Claire, on a daily basis within the classroom at another local primary where there is a special unit that he can attend for part of the day. 'He is never going to be easy,' says Anna, 'but he is at last receiving the help he needs. My advice would be, if you think your child has a problem, never give up. Why would parents want to "make up" such a thing?'

Mike and Anna's difficult experience with staff is rare, and Anna admits that there was little experience of special needs amongst the staff in the small rural school they first chose for Anthony. But their experience illustrates the need to get involved – and not give up.

Get as much information – and give as much information – about your child as possible. Ask questions. How did the problem start? When? Is it just happening in one situation or many? Is it just reading or spelling too? Is my child worried? Is the problem occurring just at school or at home too?

If you don't agree with what's being said by teachers try not to be defensive or confrontational. If the school have identified the problem they are trying to help. You need to work together. Even if you don't agree on the whys and wherefores, agree to help each other, and more importantly, your child. Keep in touch with the SENCO who will closely follow the SEN Code of Practice. This practical government document gives advice to parents, the school and all the agencies working with parents and children. It contains thorough guidelines to enable an assessment to be made and needs to be identified accurately. As a result of the 1996 Education Act, all professionals must take the code into account.

A copy of the Code of Practice can be obtained from the DfES publications department on 0845 6022260 or on the website at www.des.gov.gsl.uk/sen.

The code describes how to help children by following a 'step-by-step' or graduated procedure throughout which the school will keep you informed and involved.

Step One: called 'School Action' – the teacher will identify that a child needs extra help in the classroom.

Step Two: called 'School Action Plus' – extra help will be given, individually, or in a group with an LSA/TA or the SENCO.

If this need continues, a specialist teacher from outside the school may also be asked to assist the child, either individually or in a group.

Step Three: 'Pre-statementing' – the extra support will continue, but the child will now be regarded as needing assessment to see if a 'Statement of Special Educational Need' is required.

Step Four: Statementing. A 'statement' is drawn up, detailing those special needs.

This step-by-step approach means that a child may be removed from the Special Needs Register – which every school keeps – at any time if it appears that his needs have been met and he no longer needs special attention.

While he is on the register, a child will have a special record – often called an Individual Education Plan – which will detail the help he is getting, set targets, and dates for progress checks and review and give ideas for how parents can help at home.

The SENCO will always include parents in discussions, as their views are important.

If your child is identified as having special needs, keep talking. Don't be afraid to ask questions about things you don't understand and speak up if you don't agree with something. The SENCO may be the professional helping your child – but you are his parent.

If things don't improve, a child will be invited for assessment so that a Statement of Special Educational Need can be drawn up (Step 5). This is called 'statementing' and may be followed at a later stage by a more detailed statutory assessment, especially if it is decided that a child will be better served in a special school for children with special educational needs.

It has to be said that whatever the theory, in practice, statementing is very rare, and hard to initiate before school years Five or Six. Neither does a statement automatically mean that a child will be given a place in a special school: it just formalises the list of needs which must be met by the Local Education Authority for him to reach his full potential. Most teaching will continue in the context of mainstream schools. But very occasionally – and this depends on the policy and provision of the Local Education Authority – a child may be given a place at a special unit attached to a mainstream school, or in a special school.

The whole process of assessment, statementing and accurate provision takes some considerable time and can be enormously frustrating for parents, children and schools. It sometimes seems

'As Well as Can Be Expected'

as if nothing is moving forward. If this happens to you, talk to the SENCO. She may be able to get things moving. Keep asking anyone and everyone – teachers, governors, even local councils and MPs – about progress, to keep your child's profile in mind. Find out everything you can about process and provision. You should be kept up to date with progress and involved in all major decisions.

The sad fact is that, although *policies* for special education have moved at a fast, furious and, often, fabulous pace, *provision*, and the level of resources haven't kept up. It can still take far too long for a child to be assessed. What is recommended on paper may blow away in the winds of bureaucracy, dry up in the drought of under-resourcing or sink without trace with a change of local government policy.

As a last resort you can appeal to an SEN tribunal. (All LEAs will have details of these.)

The most important thing to remember is that your child is unique, and deserves the educational provision that will enable him to achieve his full potential, in an environment in which he can happily thrive. However long and drawn out the process of assessment and provision appears to be, remain focused on those objectives.

You may find that while you wait, much of your support will come from charities, parents' support groups and voluntary agencies appropriate to your child's difficulty.

> **Top Tip:** Find parents who have 'been there, done that' ahead of you with their own child's special needs – they can be an enormous source of encouragement and support.

A Word about Giftedness and Exceptional Ability

Many parents may not consider the needs of very bright or gifted children to be 'special'. It might seem insensitive to mention these exceptional children here. Surely they have nothing but advantages? But there can be considerable stresses, as well as privileges, for parents of these children, and isolation and frustration for the children themselves. So, gifted children are considered to have special educational needs – albeit of a very different nature.

Some children do very well at school. They thrive in an academic environment and appear to float through tests with flair and aplomb. Sometimes those children will be identified not just as being naturally academic, hardworking or 'bright', but 'gifted'. Giftedness is hard to define. But if a child excels musically or artistically, is a natural academic 'high flyer', is particularly outstanding at Mathematics, English or a Science subject, or delights in complex problem-solving, or even if he just works harder, faster and further than his peers, he may be considered to be 'gifted'.

He may find ordinary classroom tasks frustrating – often the reason why some gifted children appear to underachieve academically. He may also have problems relating to other children, show impatience with staff and generally find socialising, keeping to school routines and working within limitations extremely difficult.

But a gifted child needs to learn to work in the social environment of school just like everyone else. The school environment, in turn, should provide him with the National Curriculum enrichment and extra 'extension' work he needs to fulfil his considerable potential, whilst working alongside his classmates – albeit at a higher level and an accelerated pace.

Both parents and teachers can get advice from the National Association for Gifted Children (see Further Information at the back of this book), which offers guidance to parents and schools, and will suggest resources and further study for exceptionally able children.

'How Does a Primary School Support Pupils with Special Medical Needs?'

When a child needs regular medication, or has a serious or chronic medical problem, the school will need to know. Parents will be asked to complete a medical form with details of the family doctor, a contact telephone number and details about the administration of medication. Some children may have medical conditions (e.g. asthma, epilepsy, anaphylaxis) which, if not properly managed, could disrupt their education or put them at risk in school. These children will be regarded as having special medical needs. Most children with special medical needs will still be able to attend school regularly and, with some support from the school, will take part in most normal school activities.

Olivia received treatment in hospital as soon as her leukaemia was diagnosed. Her classmates were kept in touch with her progress, the teacher invited Olivia's Macmillan nurse into the school to explain Olivia's disease and treatment, and the children sent cards, letters and artwork to Olivia along with keeping her up to date with classroom gossip! The children were even involved in making Olivia a series of very fetching fleece hats and brightly coloured scarves to cover her chemotherapy baldness.

When Olivia's treatment was complete, the entire school population were asked to be especially careful about spreading infection, and to be on the lookout for chickenpox, which could be potentially serious for Olivia. She was able to rejoin the school community very gradually, and with the interest and support of classmates and staff, went on to make a full recovery.

Olivia's experience illustrates that even the most serious of illnesses can be handled in the school environment when awareness is raised, understanding is widespread and the correct safety precautions are taken.

'What Kind of Guidance Do Schools Receive about Medical Care and Medication?'

A DfES good practice guide for supporting pupils with special medical needs helps schools draw up policies on managing medication and offers guidelines to enable them to give effective support to children.

'As Well as Can Be Expected'

Most primary schools will have the occasional, but regular, support and attendance of a school nurse. She will sometimes be involved with a school doctor or a local GP, in an initial interview with every new entrant and his parent to assess his health and medical needs. She will be familiar with common childhood ailments, like childhood asthma, and will often oversee immunisation programmes. She may also organise the administration of any medicines children bring into school, and will delegate this responsibility to other members of learning support staff. Children will not normally, with the exception of asthma inhalers or insulin, be allowed to self-medicate. In most cases where routine antibiotics and simple medication are needed, the school will be happy to give the child the medication once a doctor's recommendation is established.

All schools will have at least one member of staff who is recently and appropriately trained to be responsible for First Aid, and they will usually be called if a child receives more than a scraped knee in the playground. First-aid provision must be available at all times while children are on school premises, and off the premises whilst on school visits.

In the case of food allergies (nuts, dairy produce, and so on) or ADHD (Attention Deficit Hyperactivity Disorder) a medical examination or report will usually be needed before arrangements for appropriate care are made. Staff may need special training to take responsibility for children with severe allergies. Sadly, such problems are becoming so common that most schools are able to take them in their stride, and will do their best to make sure a child doesn't feel 'different'.

The Parentalk Guide to Primary School

'What Happens If My Child Is Taken Ill at School?'

'Tummy pains' are a common feature of school life even when children get them in their elbow or head!

If a child is ill at school, staff will use their discretion to decide whether he needs just a little time out and the comfort of a friend, or whether parents should be contacted. For this reason it's important to make sure that the school has three up-to-date contact phone numbers (of parents, family or friends) in order of priority, for use in an emergency.

Schools have usually 'seen it all before' and will not be in the least fazed by childhood aches, pains and phobias – including the children's introduction to head-lice, threadworms and associated wriggling worries!

'Yes . . . What About All That Itching and Scratching?'

You will probably scratch your scalp at some point over the next few minutes. Because for some reason there's nothing like the mention of head-lice to get everyone itching!

Head-lice and threadworms will inevitably turn up on at least one occasion in a child's school career – and they'll usually be keen for a return visit. As visitors they are certainly nothing to be ashamed of, and are in no way a sign of bad hygiene or health – in fact, quite the opposite. It seems that head-lice go for clean, shiny healthy hair rather than grubby tresses. If you're a head-louse, why spend your visit to this new and hair-rich neighbourhood in a grubby one-star hotel when a five star with silky sheets is on offer?

'As Well as Can Be Expected'

We proved this on frequent occasions when my son, who could well have authored a booklet entitled *Sixty Reasons Not to Have a Shower*, entertained head-lice only a handful of times in his whole school career, whereas my daughter, who specialises in bathroom occupation, found they were reluctant to part from her – and always in her parting!

True, head-lice travel fast and furiously across long-haired heads locked together in girlie companionship. This might be a good reason for keeping girls' hair short or tied up, but for my daughter it did seem rather rough – and itchy – justice.

> ***Top Tip:*** *When head-lice strike, treat the whole family at home together – and that includes Mum and Dad. This should stop the lice – and you – from hopping round in circles.*

Tea Tree Oil is often an effective natural remedy for head-lice when combined with wet combing, but the school nurse or Local Health Authority will usually advise the head (ouch) teacher on current effective chemical treatments for head-lice – and for their equally itchy cousins, threadworms.

This information will be passed on to parents with general advice not to panic, and strategies to help, whenever there is an outbreak of itchies and wrigglies – very often in the summer term.

The Parentalk Guide to Primary School

All Things Teeth and Tetanus

About once a year, a dentist will visit the school for a general check of the children's teeth. No treatment will be given, but parents will be advised should there be concern about anything that is spotted in what is little more than a quick peep into an open mouth. This visit is certainly no substitute for regular visits to a family dentist.

'Will My Child Have Immunisations at School?'

Children are given a number of different immunisations at school. It is the most cost-efficient and effective way of immunising large numbers of children – and, probably, for children – the most stress-free. They can be encouraged to take immunisations in their stride, as well as in their arm.

It's a good idea to be there with them in the early years, but later in the school when children have their pre-secondary BCG or tetanus jabs – don't. There is great camaraderie in standing in a row, sleeves rolled up, with all your buddies and being brave together. It's just not cool to have Mum or Dad showing up then!

Parents are always told about risks and recommendations ahead of every immunisation programme, and, following medical advice, will have the opportunity to discuss or refuse each one.

Currently children will be offered the following immunisations at (or just before) school:

'As Well as Can Be Expected'

1. **A pre-school booster** – age 3–5 years. This protects against diphtheria, tetanus and whooping cough (DTP) in one injection.
2. **A polio booster** in drops by mouth – often with or on a sugar lump, sweet or lolly, and, if required, a second MMR injection.
3. **A BCG skin test** at around age 10–11, to detect natural immunity to TB and a follow-up injection when necessary. (This injection is often alternatively given shortly after birth in high TB risk areas.)
4. **Meningitis 'C':** (If this hasn't been given by the GP before school.) Since schools are the focus of outbreaks of meningitis 'C' it is in everyone's interests that they are protected as effectively as possible. Parents can find out more about this vaccine and others in information leaflets available from chemists, Health Visitors and GP surgeries, or on the website www.immunisation.org.uk.

Some children may also be offered another tetanus immunisation before secondary school, or if there is a chance they may have missed it earlier.

> ***Top Tip:*** *Keep a record of immunisations in your 'school' file. It's easy to forget the details – especially if your child should need an emergency tetanus jab.*

The Parentalk Guide to Primary School

If reading this last chapter has made you itch, scratch and worry – try to keep things in perspective. Before you know it you will probably have steered your child around every conceivable obstacle and from one end of primary school to the other, until the day when you suddenly realise that they are near the very end and about to begin the next part of their adventure. Life beyond eleven ...

Eleven Plus

What Comes Next?

Perhaps this chapter is more of an after word, because by the time a child is ten or eleven, most parents will feel like an old hand at 'this primary school business'.

But just as you feel as if you've got it all taped, secondary school is ahead and – to mix my metaphors thoroughly – you start to feel like an old hand trying to learn new tricks.

If you are reading this while your child is in Year Six, it might have seemed as if the year had hardly begun before the conversation at the school gate turned to the question, 'Where to next?'

The Parentalk Guide to Secondary School deals with issues related to the whole of a child's secondary school career, and you might like to dovetail the two books at this point. But I wouldn't want to wave you off into the sunset without helping you think through the options facing you and your child at the edge of that Primary Universe.

'How Do We Choose a Secondary School?'

In the autumn term of Year Six, children take a booklet home from school produced either by the Local Education Authority or the school itself which gives the key information needed to make an appropriate and informed choice of secondary school. For some, a choice is made almost immediately.

There may be a good local comprehensive for which the primary school is a 'feeder' school. It is well known, and friends, cousins or neighbours are already happily settled there. It's easy to feel that there isn't a need to look elsewhere. But just as it's advisable to look at more than one school when a child is three, four or five, it's wise to do the same when they are ten or eleven. Secondary schools usually hold 'Open Evenings' – and sometimes afternoons – to which they invite parents and prospective pupils. These are often advertised in the local press and via the primary school, and are also usually held in the autumn term of Year Six.

> **Top Tip:** As with primary schools – look at as many secondary schools as you can before making a choice.

Eleven Plus

The programme of a new entrants' evening can vary from a simple matter of a school tour and a chat from the head teacher, to an action-packed event including an opportunity to meet staff and pupils in their working environment, hear a talk from the head teacher – or be entertained by music and drama groups.

Parents can attend as many of these new entrant events as they like in order to get a good idea what individual schools have to offer.

Once again, choice of school could be restricted by catchment area, accessibility (will children from this area need to catch a school bus?) and selection procedures. So parents need to bear those in mind as they view. They should also apply that indispensable well-honed parental skill – 'reading between the lines'!

Our son whittled his choice down to two schools: a selective grammar school with a good academic reputation and traditional curriculum, and an excellent, oversubscribed, community comprehensive drawing children from a wide area.

The Open Evening at the first was, sadly, dull and disorganised. On arrival we found it difficult to park and got hopelessly lost navigating our way around a vast dark campus. Once we'd been 'found' we trooped around equally dark and dingy corridors behind a sixth form pupil with a dozen other parents passing what seemed to be dozens of empty, messy classrooms, to be shown two or three which had obviously been specially spring-cleaned and organised for the occasion. Finally, we squeezed into the school hall to hear a talk from the head teacher, which was filled with head-made statistics, rather than heartfelt welcome.

The truth was, the school community felt it didn't need to make a good impression. The head teacher knew his school was the only boys' grammar in the area, and that a large number of boys would compete for a limited number of places. The school's complacency showed – and it wasn't a pretty sight. Those parents who wanted a grammar school education at all costs stayed longest that evening. We – and several others – left, disappointed and uninspired. So did our son. He hadn't set eyes on a single computer all evening – not a good sign as far as he was concerned.

By contrast the open evening at the comprehensive school was a joy. The whole school community was involved in 'showing off' the school of which they are justifiably proud. Car parking was thoughtfully and efficiently managed by older pupils, we were given a warm and helpful welcome, and refreshments were served. Prospective pupils were allowed 'hands on' time in nearly every subject. (We came home with a jet fighter drawn on a CAD system, a printout of – I really couldn't tell you what but it excited my son – from the electronics room, and brightly coloured paper chemically patterned in the chemistry lab.)

While the children explored in small groups supervised by older pupils, we heard from the head teacher on the ethos of the school and the deputy head teachers on results, progress monitoring and pastoral care. We then chose from a number of talks on key subjects. The Head of English was so inspiring I asked my husband if I could go back to school.

There was an atmosphere of enthusiasm, teamwork, achievement, quality and fun. At the end of the evening, as it got dark, the school's steel band started playing in the quad, and parents, staff and children danced together – the atmosphere was electric.

For my son – and for us – there was no contest. Yet this was not just a gullible family taken in by a good PR job. Our impression was built out of the school's delight in what it was achieving and what it wanted to give our son, expressed by pupils and staff together – and they haven't failed us yet. Sometimes the pace of work is a little slow, but his place in extension groups for key subjects and top sets for others means he can generally work at his own speed and depth. The mix of children means he gets a flavour of a life – and language – very different to the one at home, and that's not always easy. But he has good friendships, dedicated, friendly staff who appreciate his will to work hard, and we are always welcomed in school with warmth and interest.

So think carefully about what you want from a secondary school. It's about more than results, kudos and reputation.

> ***Top Tip:*** *Secondary school is the environment in which your child will learn to be an adult. Consider carefully what kind of adult that school will teach him to be.*

'When Does a School Choose Its Pupils?'

If parents decide on a school that is 'selective', either academically or otherwise, they will need to arrange an interview and selection tests. These usually take place in the autumn term before the year in which a child will start, and are arranged by the secondary school itself, or by the LEA.

Some schools (church schools, for instance) select children whose families are church members and will want to interview both parents and children and receive a letter of recommendation from a clergy member. But the most common criteria for admission is ability, either in areas where, for historical reasons, grammar schools still remain, or because parents and child have chosen an independent school.

The exam we commonly call the '11+' isn't designed or used with Mr Butler's original 1944 purpose in mind, but remains a series of tests designed to assess whether or not your child will be able to cope with the rigours of a grammar school curriculum.

'How Do Selection Tests Work?'

Schools are allowed to administer selection procedures, including tests, following strict criteria set by the government.[4] They will use a range of tests from varying sources (for example, the National Federation for Educational Research or NFER) for selection of the most able pupils, or for pupils most suited to the style of education they offer.

Sometimes a variety of tests are used alongside an interview. Tests include verbal and non-verbal reasoning (often in multiple choice format), Mathematics skills and application, an essay and English comprehension paper, and sometimes specialist papers. Science and humanities work might also be included, and specific scholarship exams in Music or Art will require at least a performance piece or a portfolio of work.

Tests will generally be held at the school, or one of a group of schools, to which a child has made an application. This can be a daunting experience for all concerned.

When my daughter sat her selection examination for grammar school, we arrived at the exam venue – an alternative grammar school – feeling apprehensive enough. We were then shown into the school hall where hundreds of girls and their parents were clustered around the edge. As we stood waiting for the girls to be called to different classrooms to sit their tests, the sense of competition was almost tangible. More from the parents than the girls! It was an oppressive atmosphere, which did nothing to build the girls' confidence or help them to relax. I was just glad that my daughter took it in her stride, and was more interested in the Christmas shopping trip and lunch out I had planned for afterwards!

Some schools vary their tests from year to year to try to avoid pupils 'learning' how to do the tests, rather than allowing the tests to identify ability. This is a real problem for schools – but an even greater one for pupils. Many parents have such a great desire for their child to attend a grammar or selective academic school that they arrange private tutoring for months in advance of the tests, so that their child can be prepared.

'Should I Arrange Coaching for My Child?'

Whilst it's sensible to ensure that children have some familiarity with the style of tests (especially the unique style of verbal and non-verbal tests), it can be counterproductive to put them through a long and rigorous preparation period. Selection tests are designed to do just that: select. And to select for a certain style of academic education and the demands that accompany it.

'Training' children to perform well in tests only to have them flounder once they gain a place in the school and start on an academic programme is obviously damaging. It may result in the disintegration of a child's confidence, their ability – even their educational future. Like Chloe. She spent every Thursday evening at tutorials to prepare for her selection tests. She 'learnt' to do the tests she would face, and had hours of practice. Her parents were delighted when she passed her exams and took up her place at a very academic grammar school. But she floundered from day one, unable to keep up with the volume of work or the intellectual demands it made on her.

The school did everything possible to support her, but inevitably made the decision that she would be better off moving to another school more suited to her learning style and ability. It was a tremendous blow to Chloe. Her parents were wonderful and, despite their disappointment, did everything they could to counteract the sense of failure and rejection Chloe felt. She is now just beginning her GCSE courses at a good comprehensive school – but damage has been done. Chloe's mum reports that they are on a daily mission to restore her self-esteem and encourage her to do her best. Chloe is very slowly recognising the advantages of being in a school where she can really excel. It may not be too late for a turnaround, but the journey has been – and might still be – a painful one.

However bright and keen your ten-year-old is, ask the advice of his class teacher before you send him down the selective test route. She will know whether he is intellectually capable, not just of doing well in the tests, but of the particular style and pace of work beyond them and, like you, will want him to do his best. If you're not convinced by her response, get a second opinion from another teacher or tutor. But either way consider the route ahead carefully.

You may also need to consider whether you might be denying an academically capable child the opportunities offered by a rigorous academic curriculum by choosing not to consider a school with selective entry. Much will depend on your local provision and your personal beliefs.

> **Top Tip:** Choose a secondary school to fit your child – don't try to make your child fit the school.

Whichever school you choose, be guided by your child's ability, gifts and needs. Resist the pressure to get him into a 'good school' where he might struggle, and turn a sceptical ear to the expectations of family and friends to that end. You know your child best. It is important that he attends a school where he will be happy, can thrive and will be encouraged to be the best that he can be – and not just academically.

The Last Term of All...

So, you've reached the last term at primary school. How far off does that buggy at the edge of the playground seem now? As Granny often says, 'Haven't they grown?'

The Parentalk Guide to Primary School

But there may be other changes too. Year Six children often begin to feel that schoolwork is less demanding, and often display restlessness and a desire for change, challenge and new opportunities.

It may be now – especially with girls – that self-doubt begins in earnest. A few more doors begin to slam intentionally. Tempers may begin to flare a little more unpredictably than before and, as parents, you find yourselves thinking, 'Where did that come from?' as your child's verbal explosion subsides!

On the other hand, it may be a few more years before it's obvious that there's an adolescent in the house. Either way, batten down the hatches and get ready *now*.

'Help! There's an Adolescent on the Way – What Can I Do?'

Around about the time of leaving primary school is not a bad time to reflect, not just on the school years, but on your parenting – a kind of Parenting MOT. So take some time out with and without your child to review how things are going, what his needs are, and how you can begin to give him a little more of the independence he'll need to learn to handle responsibly, as the teenage years hurtle towards all of you.

- Look at the behaviour boundaries, privileges and responsibilities you have given your child, and decide whether he needs the elastic of independence to be gradually stretched.
- Decide which skills he may need to begin secondary school – and start building them now. Will he need to travel on a

bus? Has he developed some 'streetwise' skills? What's his road sense like?
- Can he find his way around the locality in relative safety and on foot – or do you always taxi him everywhere by car?
- How does he handle money? Should you consider changing his allowance or giving him independent use of a young person's bank account?
- Listen to his views and ideas – take some time to get to know his world. Ask yourself: Do I know his best friends' names? His favourite band? His gifts and abilities, weaknesses and fears? How does he deal with stress? What does he like to do to relax or celebrate?
- Be available to listen – and talk – whenever possible. Offer to spend time one to one and give him the opportunity to share any concerns about the forthcoming school change. Maybe take him out for a pizza, and just make the most of the time to chat – and not *just* about school.
- Talk to friends who've been down the road before you about their experiences – without expecting your child to be the same. Read a book on preparing to parent teenagers (see Further Information) – but don't just sit there waiting for it all to happen!

There will inevitably be storms – at the very least little squalls – ahead. But this period is also an exciting one for parents, as they watch their child change into a young adult and, ultimately and hopefully, a friend.

Leaving primary school is the first step.

The Parentalk Guide to Primary School

Leaving Primary School

Emotions are often frayed and fragile as the last week of the last term arrives. It's an important step – not just for your child but for you as a parent too. Suddenly you'll have one eye on that distant day when they'll fly the nest forever. And you'll now know from the experience you've gained over the primary years, that such a day isn't quite as distant as it appears. It will come all too quickly.

> **Top Tip:** *The last term at primary school is often an emotional box of fireworks for children – expect some behaviour to match!*

One of my fondest memories as a parent includes the day of my daughter's primary school 'Leavers' Disco'. It was a simple, early-evening affair based in the school hall – but a Big Event, for all concerned. She invited a large group of her friends to meet at our home beforehand to eat pizza, giggle and generally make the most of it all. They chose outfits, fiddled with each other's hair, and helped each other to get ready – a sign of things to come! Just before they left, dressed in their finery and on a high, they all sat on the bottom of the stairs in a huddle of arms and hugs for some photographs to be taken. With ten different cameras I took dozens of shots of those giggling pink-faced females prettily dressed. Not quite little girls any more, and not quite young women.

Eleven Plus

As I snapped away they began to sing the theme song from the USA sitcom *Friends:* 'I'll Be There for You'. It was corny, juvenile, maybe sentimental – but it was incredibly moving. I had a lump in my throat.

I waved them off as they meandered down the street together arm in arm, giggling and shrieking. I watched them turn the corner in the distance and was amused that I could still hear them shrieking as I walked back up the path to the house. I went inside, shut the door – and promptly burst into tears! Those tears were a strange mix of joy and sadness. I just realised that it was a special day. A turning point. So did my daughter.

Now, six years later, she still keeps that photograph in a special 'Friends' frame on her bookshelf. She often refers to the moment it was taken. To the optimism and excitement. Most of those smiling friends went to different schools, some she still sees occasionally. But the memory of that day will, I believe, be with her always.

The Last Day – Leaving It All Behind

Building memories is one of the best bits of being a parent – and this is the day to get out your figurative trowel and cement!

'What Can We Do to "Mark" the Last Day at School?'
Children often take an old school shirt to school on which to collect signatures, or a notebook to collect farewell messages from teachers and classmates. Even if the shirt gets thrown out

The Parentalk Guide to Primary School

by the end of the summer holiday and the notebook gets lost, they should be encouraged – it's an important part of making the transition.

Children can get very emotional about the whole event, and teachers often have their work cut out stopping the hysteria from spreading, so parents will also need to give a gentle warning not to take it all too seriously and to have a fun day rather than a tragic one! They *will* see their friends again, the school will *not* disappear via spontaneous combustion by the August Bank Holiday, and it's not *just* the end – but the beginning.

Children generally like to give a small gift to their close friends and teacher. It is also an ideal time for parents to send a letter to the class teacher and head teacher to say 'thank you' for all they, and the wider school community, have done.

Some schools encourage the donation of books to the school library in 'memory' of a leaver, or ask for financial contributions from leavers for a specific purpose – a piece of equipment or another resource that the school would benefit from. It is then marked with their school year or individual names.

Above all, find a positive way to leave something behind – and to move on.

'What Do They Take with Them When They Leave?'

Personal Records of Attainment and Achievement
Once at secondary school children will be required to build up a Progress File to review their achievements and record their

goals. Primary schools are not *required* to do this, but most children leave primary school having compiled a similar folder containing a cross-section of their work selected with the guidance of their teacher. This may or may not be passed on to their secondary school to support their 'End of Key Stage' results. Either way they will probably eventually be able to keep it as a memento of their primary education.

Mementoes

Most primary schools will arrange for a class photograph – often alongside an individual photograph – to be taken of 'leavers'. Some produce tea towels, mugs, or find even more creative ways of giving the children something special to remind them of their primary years.

One of our local schools gives each leaver a videotape containing snippets of all the major school events they've enjoyed since joining the infant classes. Whatever else they

The Parentalk Guide to Primary School

leave with – the most important thing will be those good memories.

Backward Glance...

It's not just the children who find leaving primary school a wrench. It's a milestone for parents too, especially if the child who's leaving is the last or only child.

Suddenly there'll be no more waiting at the school gate. No end of term Christmas Nativity plays, no egg and spoon sports days. Somehow it all gets a lot more serious from now on.

Our involvement with a school will probably never be quite as immediate and personal again. Primary school, we will have discovered, is a unique community. Our farewell may also herald changes in our own family life. 'No More Playground' syndrome really is a prelude to Empty Nest syndrome!

It's as if a familiar chapter of a book is ended, and we're not quite sure if we want to begin the next. But that new chapter is also the beginning of the next stage of the adventure, both for our child and for us – and we can't follow the adventure unless we turn the page . . .

Notes

1. An urban school myth adapted from Rob Parsons' *The Sixty Minute Mother* (Hodder & Stoughton, 2000).
2. Schools will provide hot lunches and/or space for children to eat packed lunches. Children whose parents receive Income Support, Income-based Job Seekers Allowance or support under Part VI of the Immigration and Asylum Act 1999 are entitled to free school meals.
3. The requirements for school reports are contained in the Pupil Information Regulations 2000 which can be obtained from www.hmso.gov.uk.
4. The School Admissions Code of Practice contains details. It can be found on the website: www.dfes.gov.uk/sacode/main.shtml. Or contact the DfES for details.

What It All Means: A Glossary of Terms in Primary Education

Attainment target
Fundamental part of a subject being studied (in English an attainment target would be reading).

Attainment levels
The levels towards which children work in each attainment target, and throughout each Key Stage. (Noted as Level One, Level Two, etc.)

Baseline assessment
A simple task-based test given to new entrants, which sets the 'baseline' for future learning.

The Parentalk Guide to Primary School

Catchment area
The LEA designated area from which a school generally takes its pupils.

County primary schools
Schools for children aged 5–11 years, wholly funded and maintained by the LEA.

Core subjects
The heart of the National Curriculum: English, Maths, Science, IT and RE (which has a special status as a core subject).

Curriculum
'The content of children's formal learning' – i.e. what they spend all day doing.

DfES
The Department for Education and Skills – the Government's education department – formerly the Department for Education and Employment/Science.

Early education settings
Pre-schools, playgroups and nurseries.

End of Key Stage Tests
Tests at ages 7 and 11, which assess children's progress within Key Stages One and Two. Commonly called SATS.

Feeder school
A primary school which traditionally or locally 'feeds' its children into a specific secondary school.

What It All Means: A Glossary of Terms in Primary Education

First School
Schools admitting pupils mainly aged 4–8 years forming the first part of a three-tier system of education.

Foundation class
The class which children join when entering school at age 4 or 5 years. Formerly called the Reception class.

Foundation subject
Other subjects making up the National Curriculum: History, Geography, Design Technology, Art, Music, PE, PHSE and Citizenship.

Grammar schools
Schools – mainly state schools, although some independent schools also have the 'grammar' title – which have 'selective entry' on the basis of an academic entrance test.

Independent school
A fee-paying school, largely outside the control of the LEA.

Infant school or department
For children aged 4–7 years.

INSET
In-Service Education and Training for teachers – also called Professional Development.

Junior school or department
For children aged 7–11years. (A primary school in England

and Wales consists of both infant and junior departments on one site.)

Key Stage
Key Stages One and Two are the first two stages of the National Curriculum, covered in primary schools.

LEA
Local Education Authority – a local government body responsible for providing education locally, and for giving administrative and advisory support to early education settings, schools and colleges.

Literacy Hour
A compulsory session of English teaching and part of the Government's National Literacy Strategy.

LSA
Learning Support Assistant – a teaching assistant working alongside the teacher, often supporting children with special needs. Also called a TA.

MTA
Meal Time Assistant – the 'dinner ladies' of old.

Middle School
For pupils aged 9–13 years, usually where pupils have attended First School. Middle School is the second tier of a three-tier system used in some parts of England and Wales.

What It All Means: A Glossary of Terms in Primary Education

National Curriculum
The basic curriculum framework setting out what children should learn in England and Wales.

NCPTA
National Confederation of Parent Teacher Associations.

NFER
National Federation for Educational Research.

NQT
Newly qualified teacher.

Numeracy Hour
A compulsory session of Mathematics teaching, arranged much like Literacy Hour.

OFSTED
The Office of Standards in Education – the schools inspection body of England and Wales (Scotland have their own inspectorate).

PGCE
Post Graduate Certificate in Education – a postgraduate teaching qualification.

Phonics
A term generally applied to the method of teaching reading and spelling through the 'sounds' that words make.

The Parentalk Guide to Primary School

PTA
Parent Teacher Association – based in schools.

SATS
End of Key Stage Tests at ages 7 and 11.

Selective schools
Schools which 'select' pupils through entrance tests or other criteria.

SEN
Special Educational Needs.

SENCO
Special Educational Needs Co-ordinator – a teacher with responsibility for special educational needs within the primary school.

SEN Code of Practice
A guide for early education settings, schools and LEAs on the help they can give special needs children.

Supply teacher
A 'relief' teacher drawn from the LEA pool.

TA
A Teaching Assistant working alongside a class teacher in a supporting role.

What It All Means: A Glossary of Terms in Primary Education

Voluntary Aided (VA)
Schools founded – and largely controlled by – a voluntary body. Aided schools often have a church affiliation and are 'Church Schools' (RC – Roman Catholic, or C of E – Church of England).

Voluntary Controlled (VC)
Refers to schools fully maintained by an LEA but which a voluntary body originally founded. Often 'Church Schools'.

Further Information

Parentalk
PO Box 23142
London SE1 0ZT

Tel: 020 7450 9073
Fax: 020 7450 9060
e-mail: info@parentalk.co.uk
Website: www.parentalk.co.uk

Provides a range of resources and services designed to inspire parents to enjoy parenthood.

Government Departments

In England:
The Department for Education and Skills – DfES
Great Smith Street
London SW1P 3BT

Tel: 0870 000 2288
Fax: 01928 794248
e-mail: info@dfes.gsi.gov.uk
Website: www.dfes.gov.uk

The DfES website has excellent links for parents, teachers and children, and a wealth of information on all aspects of school life from uniform to university. It also offers helpful guidelines on how parents can help children with key skills.

DfES Parents Gateway
Website: www.dfes.gov.uk/parents

Contains direct links to the Parents' Centre and other related websites.

The Parentalk Guide to Primary School

In Scotland:
The Scottish Executive Education Department
Victoria Quay
Edinburgh EH6 6QQ

Tel: 0131 244 0911
Enquiry line: 08457 741741
e-mail: ceu@scotland.gov.uk
Website: www.scotland.gov.uk

This deparment is the first port of call for further information on education in Scotland.

In Wales:
The Education Department
National Assembly for Wales
Crown Building
Cathays Park
Cardiff CF10 3NQ

Tel: 029 2082 5111

Gives details of local variations of provision and curriculum for Wales, e.g. Welsh language teaching.

In Northern Ireland:
Department of Education
Rathgael House
43 Balloo Road
Bangor
County Down BT19 7PR

Tel: 028 9127 9279
Fax: 028 9127 9100
e-mail: mail@deni.gov.uk
Website: www.deni.gov.uk

Organisations

Advisory Centre for Education (ACE) Ltd
1C Aberdeen Studios
22 Highbury Grove
London N5 2DQ

Tel: 020 7354 8318
Advice Line: 0808 8000 5793
e-mail: ace-ed@easynet.co.uk
Website: www.ace-ed.org.uk

Is working for an open and accountable education system that supports all children. ACE is the only independent national education advice service that provides advice and support for parents of children in state schools.

British Association for Early Childhood Education
136 Cavell Street
London E1 2SA

Tel: 020 7539 5400
e-mail: office@early-education.org.uk
Website: www.early-education.org.uk

Campaign for Learning
19 Buckingham Street
London WC2N 6EF

Tel: 020 7930 1111
Fax: 020 7930 1551

Further Information

e-mail: gphyall@cflearning.org.uk
Website: www.campaign-for-learning.org.uk

A national charity working to create an appetite for learning in individuals that will sustain them throughout their lives.

Care for the Family
PO Box 488
Cardiff CF15 7YY

Tel: 029 2081 0800
Fax: 029 2081 4089
e-mail: mail@cff.org.uk
Website: www.care-for-the-family.org.uk

Provides support for families through seminars, resources and special projects.

Citizens' Advice Bureau (CAB)
Website: www.nacab.org.uk/

A free and confidential service giving information and advice on topics such as benefits; maternity rights; debts; housing, consumer, employment and legal problems; family and personal difficulties. It also has details of useful national and local organisations. Ask at your local library or look in your phone book for your nearest office. Opening times may vary.

Contact-A-Family
209–211 City Road
London EC1V 1JN

Helpline: 0808 808 3555
Tel: 020 7608 8700
Fax: 020 7608 8701
e-mail: info@cafamily.org.uk
Website: www.cafamily.org.uk

Brings together families whose children have disabilities.

Education Extra
17 Old Ford Road
London E2 9PL

Tel: 020 8709 9900
Fax: 020 8709 9933
e-mail: info@educationextra.org.uk
Website: www.educationextra.org.uk

Supports out-of-school-hours learning.

Education Otherwise
PO Box 7420
London N9 9SG

Tel: 0870 730 0074
e-mail: enquiries@education-otherwise.org
Website: www.education-otherwise.org

Provides support and information for families whose children are being educated outside school.

The Parentalk Guide to Primary School

Gingerbread
7 Sovereign Close
Sovereign Court
London E1W 3HW

Advice line: 0800 018 4318
Tel: 020 7488 9300
Fax: 020 7488 9300
e-mail: office@gingerbread.org.uk
Website: www.gingerbread.org.uk

Provides day-to-day support and practical help for lone parents.

National Association of Gifted Children
Suite 14
14 Sherwood House
Bletchley
Bucks MK3 6DP

Tel: 0870 770 3217
e-mail: amazingchildren@nagc
  britain.org.uk
Website: www.nagcbritain.org.uk

National Autistic Society
393 City Road
London EC1V 1NG

Autism helpline: 0870 600 8585
  (Mon–Fri 10 a.m.–4 p.m.; your
  call is logged on to an answer-
  phone and the relevant regional
  volunteer will call you back)
Tel: 020 7833 2299
e-mail: nas@nas.org.uk or autism
  helpline@nas.org.uk

Website: www.nas.org.uk

Exists to champion the rights and interests of all people with autism and to ensure that they and their families receive quality services appropriate to their needs.

National Children's Bureau
8 Wakley Street
London WC1V 7QE

Tel: 020 7843 6000
Fax: 020 7278 9512
e-mail: membership@ncb.org.uk
Website: www.ncb.org.uk

A registered charity that promotes the interests and well-being of all children and young people across every aspect of their lives.

National Council for One Parent Families
255 Kentish Town Road
London NW5 2LX

Lone Parent Line: 0800 018 5026
  (Mon–Fri 9.15 a.m.–5.15 p.m.)
Maintenance & Money Line: 020
  7428 5424 (Mon & Thurs 11
  a.m.–2 p.m.; Tues 3–6 p.m.)
General enquiries: 020 7428 5400
e-mail: info@oneparentfamilies.
  org.uk
Website: www.oneparentfamilies.
  org.uk

An information service for lone parents.

Further Information

National Family and Parenting Institute
430 Highgate Studios
53–79 Highgate Road
London NW5 1TL

Tel: 020 7424 3460
Fax: 020 7485 3590
e-mail: info@nfpi.org
Website: www.nfpi.org

An independent charity set up to provide a strong national focus on parenting and families in the twenty-first century.

National Governors' Council
Lonsdale House
52 Blucher Street
Birmingham B1 1QU

Tel: 0121 616 5104
Fax: 0121 616 5105
e-mail: ngc@ngc.org.uk
Website: www.ngc.org.uk

The National Governors' Council exists to promote the views of school governing bodies and to support and develop the work they do on behalf of the community.

National Reading Campaign
National Literacy Trust
Swire House
59 Buckingham Gate
London SW1E 6AJ

Tel: 020 7828 2435

e-mail: contact@literacytrust.org.uk
Website: www.literacytrust.org.uk

NCPTA (National Confederation of Parent Teacher Associations)
18 St Johns Hill
Sevenoaks
Kent TN13 3NP

Tel: 01732 748850
e-mail: info@ncpta.org.uk
Website: www.ncpta.org.uk

NSPCC
Weston House
42 Curtain Road
London EC2A 3NH

Helpline: 0800 800 5000
Tel: 020 7825 2500
Fax: 020 7825 2525
Website: www.nspcc.org.uk

NSPCC is the UK's leading charity specialising in child protection and the prevention of cruelty to children. It is the only children's charity in the UK with the statutory powers enabling it to act to safeguard children at risk.

OFSTED (The Office for Standards in Education)
Alexandra House
33 Kingsway
London WC2B 6SE

Tel: 020 7421 6800

The Parentalk Guide to Primary School

Fax: 020 7421 6707
e-mail: geninfo@ofsted.gov.uk
Website: www.ofsted.gov.uk

OFSTED is a non-ministerial government department that manages the system of school inspection.

Parenting Education & Support Forum
Unit 431 Highgate Studios
53–79 Highgate Road
London NW5 1TL

Tel: 020 7284 8370
Fax: 020 7485 3587
e-mail: pesf@dial.pipex.com
Website: www.parenting-forum.org.uk

Aims to raise awareness of the importance of parenting and its impact on all aspects of child development.

Parentline Plus
Third Floor, Chapel House
18 Hatton Place
London EC1N 8RU

Tel: 020 7209 2460
Fax: 020 7209 2461
e-mail: headoffice@parentlineplus.org.uk
Website: www.parentlineplus.org.uk

A UK registered charity that offers support to anyone parenting a child.

Parents Information Network (PIN)
PO Box 16394
London SE1 3ZP

Tel: 020 7357 9078
Fax: 020 7357 9077
e-mail: editor@pin.org.uk
Website: www.pin-parents.com

Provides information and advice to parents whose children are using computers and the Internet.

REACH
California Country Park
Nine Mile Ride
Finchampstead
Berkshire RG40 4HT

Tel: 0118 973 7105

National advice centre for children with reading difficulties.

Young Minds
102–108 Clerkenwell Road
London EC1M 5SA

Tel: 020 7336 8445
Fax: 020 7335 8446
e-mail: enquiries@youngminds.org.uk
Website: www.youngminds.org.uk

Young Minds is the children's mental health charity.

Further Information

Further Reading

On the school curriculum
'The Learning Journey Guide' published by the DfES (see details below).

On fast-approaching teenagers
The Parentalk Guide to the Teenage Years by Steve Chalke (Hodder & Stoughton, 2000)

Get Out of My Life – But First Take Me and Alex into Town *by Tony Wolf and Suzanne Franks (Profile Books, 2002)*

On sex education
The Parentalk Guide to your Child and Sex by Steve Chalke (Hodder & Stoughton, 2000)

On secondary school
The Parentalk Guide to Secondary School (Hodder & Stoughton, out in 2003!)

Activities and Resources

Websites to explore with children:

www.bbc.co.uk (a wealth of diversions from the BBC)
www.nhm.ac.uk (The Natural History Museum)

The Parentalk Guide to Primary School

www.nmsi.ac.uk (The Science Museum)
www.holoworld.com (a site that specialises in holograms)

For maths puzzles
www.nrich.maths.org.uk/primary/index.html (developed by Cambridge University Maths students and updated each week with puzzles and posers)
www.counton.org.uk

For science
www.howstuffworks.com
www.scienceyear.com
www.frontiersclub.org.uk

For books
www.boox.org.uk
www.booktrust.org.uk
www.rif.org.uk

For education
www.dfes.gov.uk/parents
A great resource. The DfES also provide a number of resources packs to help your child with reading and maths and 'The Learning Journey Guides' – a series of free booklets to help parents understand what their children are learning and why.

Further Information

It also produces an excellent magazine for parents, *Parents and Schools*, available directly from the DfES or at supermarkets and family stores or via the Freefone number 0800 389 3899.

www.schoolsnet.com
A similar independent site containing a wealth of information on schools and school activities, advice for parents and fun and games for children.

www.tigerchild.com
A lively and original site, linked to Amazon, which has information on everything from school tables to health advice and parental rights.

More About Parentalk

Launched in 1999, in response to research, which revealed that 1 in 3 parents feel like failures, Parentalk is all about inspiring parents to make the most of their vitally important role.

A registered charity, we exist to provide relevant information and advice for mums and dads in a format that they feel most comfortable with, regardless of their background or family circumstances.

Our current activities include:

- **The Parentalk Parenting Principles Course**
  Already used by almost 25,000 mums and dads, this video-based resource brings together groups of parents to share their experiences, laugh together and learn from one another. Filmed at the studios of GMTV, endorsed by the National Confederation of Parent Teacher Associations and featuring Parentalk Founder Steve Chalke, the course is suitable for use by groups of parents in their own homes or by schools, PTAs, pre-schools and nurseries, health visitors, health centres, family centres, employers, churches and other community groups.

- **Parentalk Local Events**
  Looking at every age group from the toddler to the teenage years, and from how to succeed as a parent to how to succeed

as a grandparent, Parentalk evenings are a specially tailored, fun mixture of information, shared stories and advice for success as a mum, dad or grandparent. Operating across the country, the Parentalk team of speakers can also provide input on a range of more specialist subjects such as helping your child sleep or striking a healthy balance between work and family life.

- **Parentalk at Work Events**
Parentalk offer lunchtime and half-day workshops for employers and employees, at their place of work, that look at getting the balance right between the responsibilities of work and those of a family. Parentalk also provides a life coaching service for employees, helping them to deal with the pressures they encounter at home in order to be happier, and perform better, at work.

  All Parentalk at Work initiatives are backed up by a comprehensive website: **www.parentalk.co.uk/atwork**

- **The Parentalk Guide Series**
In addition to the 'How to Succeed' series, Parentalk offers a comprehensive series of titles that look at a wide variety of parenting issues. All of these books are easy-to-read, down-to-earth and full of practical information and advice.

- **The Parentalk Schools Pack**
This resource, designed especially for year 9 pupils, builds on the success of the Parentalk Video Course, to provide material for eight lessons on subjects surrounding preparing for parenthood. The pack has been tailored to dovetail with

More About Parentalk

the PHSE and citizenship curriculum and is available for teachers to download from the Parentalk website.

- **www.parentalk.co.uk**
www.parentalk.co.uk is a lively, upbeat site exclusively for parents, packed with fun ideas, practical advice and some great tips for making the most of being a mum or dad.

To find out more about any of these Parentalk initiatives or our plans for the future, or to receive our quarterly newsletter, contact a member of the team at the address below:

Parentalk
115 Southwark Bridge Road
London SE1 0AX
Tel: 020 7450 9073
Fax: 020 7450 9060
e-mail: info@parentalk.co.uk

Parentalk

Helping parents make the most of every stage of their child's growing up.

(Registered Charity No: 1074790)